LARRY AUSTIN
Life and Works of an Experimental Composer

Borik Press Studies of Composers (1)
Series Editor: Rodney Waschka II

LARRY AUSTIN
Life and Works of an Experimental Composer

Thomas S. Clark

Borik Press

Borik Press
P.O. Box 12784
Raleigh, North Carolina, 27605
USA

Borik Press and its logo, a digital tree symbol, are trademarks of Borik Press.

Larry Austin: Life and Works of an Experimental Composer
Copyright 2012 Thomas Clark

All rights reserved. No part of this publication may be reproduced stored in a retrieval system, or transmitted, in any form or by any means, electronic, mechanical, photocopying, recording, or any information storage or retrieval system, or otherwise, without the prior permission of Borik Press.

This book is sold subject to the condition that it shall not, by way of trade or otherwise, be lent, re-sold, hired out or otherwise circulated without the publisher's prior consent in any form of binding or cover other than that in which it is published and without a similar condition including this condition being imposed on the subsequent purchaser.

Printed in the United States of America.
ISBN: 978-0-9855654-0-4

CONTENTS

PREFACE vii

LARRY AUSTIN'S LIFE
Early Texas years 1
Student composer 4
Military and marriage 6
California 7
Student composer again 8
MacDowell Colony, Bernstein 11
Improvisation 12
Rome 13
Hosting Stockhausen and Cage 15
SOURCE magazine 16
Florida Years 19
Later Texas years 20
CDCM 22
International travel and residencies 23
Academic career coda 24

LARRY AUSTIN'S WORK
What kind of composer are you? 27
Improvisation 28
Homage variations 29
Beyond Pierrot 30
Ives' Universe Symphony 32
Remixing Cage 37
Mapping, fractals 39
More fractals 42
Other models 44
Computer Music 47
Convolutions 52
Ambisonics 54
Conversations 55
Specific soloists 58

THE EXPERIMENTAL COMPOSER
Experiments in medium and materials 61
Octophonics, convolutions, homages 62
Experiments in notation 63

Experiments in improvisation and form   65
Impact and influence   67

INFORMATION

ENDNOTES   69
LARRY AUSTIN TIMELINE   71
COMPOSITIONS
Large instrumental ensembles   77
Chamber Ensembles   79
Soloist with tape/electronics   81
Tape/computer music   85
Instrumental solo/duo   87
Chorus/opera/voice   87
RECORDINGS
Compact discs   89
Other media   95
BOOKS, CHAPTERS, PERIODICALS   97
ARTICLES
by Austin   98
co-authored   104
OTHER SOURCES   105
INDEX   107
ABOUT THE AUTHOR   117

PREFACE

It seems impossible to tell the story of a composer's life and a composer's work without recognizing how the two threads intertwine and become one. In this book I will not attempt to unravel this tapestry, not only because it would be difficult and counter-productive, but precisely because my interest is drawn toward the broadest horizon of the creative process. It is important not only to ask where a particular composition came from, what were the sources of materials, the kernel concept, and the intent of the work, but where the composer came from, literally and more metaphorically in terms of life experiences, non-musical interests, values, and way of viewing and observing the world.

Why then a book connecting the life and musical works of Larry Austin in particular? There are two reasons, one simple, the other more complex. In the spirit of full disclosure, I have a fundamental bias: Larry is a great friend, a person I enjoy, admire, and love. That's the simple reason: to follow the old adage and write about what you know and what interests you. The more complex reason is how I consider his music: it has covered so much fascinating sonic and intellectual ground. His career has ranged from traditional orchestra and chamber music mediums to avant garde improvisation, to electronic pioneering, to the most cutting edge advances in computer music. In each of these, he has accomplished three things: 1) become a highly proficient practitioner; 2) become a recognized leader exploring new ideas; and 3) made pieces that pose stimulating challenges for performers and intriguing sonic experiences for listeners.

Throughout this book, biographical facts will be interlaced with Austin's personal quotes, opinions, and my observations. If reading it ends up feeling like listening to a conversational dialog, that's not a coincidence. Larry Austin and I wrote a book together in the nineteen eighties, *Learning to Compose*. Our working style of collaboration consisted mainly of long conversations (usually over lunch on the University of North Texas campus) that forged the essential ideas and approaches of what we intended to be a groundbreaking exploration of the process of composing. We decided on the same approach for this book, not only as a working style we found productive but also, we would both confess, as an excuse to resume these enjoyable conversations.

The *Life and Works* conversations started August 4, 2003. Most occurred again over lunch, this time at Robson Ranch, a senior living community Larry and Edna Austin chose as their retirement residence over rather different retirement options such as New York City. The club house at Robson Ranch is on a hill with a serene vista of wide-open Texas prairie. I think of these conversations as an ongoing series I do not wish to see end. The more recent ones directed toward the writing of this book took place in August 2005, July 2007, and in 2010 leading up to the celebration of his 80th birthday in Denton.

Larry Austin is both a friend and a fascinating person. I admire him as a colleague who has led the field of musical inquiry and innovation in important organizational roles. And I have learned a lot as a composer from his imaginative, ingenious compositions, the pioneering musical ideas they embody, and the working methods of their creation. It has been a great partnership.

Acknowledgment of those who contributed to the writing of this book must first go to Larry himself – for entrusting me with the writing of his authorized biography; for his wit and excellent memory; and in particular for his industrious organization of his own work. His personal web site, cemi.music.unt.edu/larry_austin, provided much of the information for the lists of works, recordings, etc., as well as program notes for all of his major works.

His former student, our colleague, friend and publisher Rodney Waschka of Borik Press, must be thanked for his encouragement and his own insights into the significance of Larry Austin's work. I also received encouragement and critical writing advice from my patient spouse, professional editor extraordinaire Elizabeth Clark.

Finally, I want to recognize Edna Austin for being such a great life partner supporting Larry's career, and thank her for letting me spend so much time with her devoted husband. I had the honor of being with both of them on a sunny, cool, perfect November day in 2003, a late autumn Saturday afternoon at Robson Ranch shortly after our book conversations had begun. Their home was filled with people, children running around, adults clustered around the food spread out on the kitchen island, older folks seated in various corners chatting quietly. It was a family reunion of sorts, but the focus of attention became drawn to a DVD slide show playing in the family room. Shots of parents and children visiting Italy, standing together by fountains, in plazas with strollers; more scenes of backyard cookouts in California, family pets, friends visiting for parties. This digital album assembled by their adult children was a fiftieth wedding anniversary gift celebrating the marriage in 1953 of Edna Navarro and Larry Austin. It too has been a great partnership.

- Thomas Clark, 2011

1943

Austin, front row, second from left, youngest member of the Vernon High School Band brass sextet, attending Texas state competition at North Texas State Teachers College, Denton

LARRY AUSTIN'S LIFE

Early Texas years

Learning to play an instrument in a public school band is one common way for a young person in America to discover music. The 1940s were war years in which military bands were prevalent and popular across the country. And so it was in Vernon, a small Texas community near the Panhandle. But the inspiration to a musical life was a bit different for one young boy growing up there.

"My ninth birthday was approaching, and my mother asked me what gift I wanted from my parents." Larry Austin recalls his response: "A trombone, just like my grandfather Slim played." Clarence "Slim" Newburn had been a self-taught trombonist and violinist playing in vaudeville orchestras on tour in Texas and Oklahoma. "My mother understood my wish completely and took me to the local music teacher, Paul Goetze, in Vernon. Mr. Goetze advised us that my arms were as yet too short to play the trombone."

Instead, Goetze recommended purchasing a used trumpet for $32, a price that included weekly lessons at 25 cents each. "My mother 'paid down' five dollars for the trumpet, and we took it home. Every week I would bike over to Mr. Goetze's home for my lesson with the trumpet case hanging from the handlebars." He studied with Mr. Goetze for the next year, as his parents paid the monthly installments on the instrument. He continued on his own, performing almost every Sunday in church, playing anthems from the hymnal.

In 1941, E.W. Sheppard directed the Vernon High School band. Word reached him about a precocious sixth-grade trumpeter, whom he drafted at age 11 to play with the high school band. Austin was given special permission to leave his elementary school each day and go over to the high school for 11 a.m. rehearsals with Mr. Sheppard's high school band. Clearly, Austin was eager and musically gifted.

Austin was six years old when his family moved to Vernon. Born September 12, 1930, in Duncan, Oklahoma (his mother had been born in Chickasha, his father in Copperas Cove, Texas), he recalls that crossing the Red River and moving to Texas "was a big deal" for the family. His parents eventually retired to Lake Texoma, on the border of the two states. Much later, in 1965 as he was in Rome on sabbatical from the University of California-Davis, a letter was forwarded to him from an Oklahoma woman wanting to know why composers would leave Oklahoma. "Well, it wasn't up to me" was his answer.

In Vernon, young Austin also played second trumpet in a student sextet for a contest held at North Texas State Teachers College in Denton. (Located north of Fort Worth and Dallas, the school has changed names several times: to North Texas State College, then North Texas State University, then University of North Texas, or UNT. It will be referred to as "North Texas".) Austin says he "was in awe" of the experience playing on the stage of NTSTC's Main Auditorium, a large barn-like hall with a balcony and broad proscenium. (The hall still sees limited use.) The School of Music at North Texas had a great reputation, especially for opera. Austin recalls an entire opera production directed by Mary McCormick performed in the Vernon High School auditorium.

Not surprisingly, when it was time for college in 1947, Austin headed to Denton to study music at North Texas. That happened to be a significant year, in which the very first "dance band" was formed there. This was the earliest ancestor of what is now the world famous UNT One O'Clock Lab Band, and the first step in what would later become the leading jazz studies program in the world.

Flash-forward to the end of the century, as the jazz studies program celebrated its fiftieth anniversary, Austin posed for a commemorative photo at the reunion with fellow pioneer "jazzers," surviving charter members of that first group. Back in 1947, these were excellent student musicians, many of them in fact veterans of military bands going to college on the GI Bill.

Austin sensed, "It was in the air that this was something important."

But jazz was yet to be offered as a major, so Austin chose to study music education. Maurice McAdow, who gave Austin some cornet lessons, was the concert band director. Able-bodied wind and percussion players were expected to be in the marching band, but Austin was "sick of it" from high school. He quickly got a medical excuse for infected poison ivy. But not being in the marching band didn't win any points with Professor McAdow for getting into the concert band, so Austin auditioned for orchestra, directed by George Morey (also a composer and flute teacher). He got in, joining a trumpet section with Euell Box, who went on to a successful career as a composer for films such as "Benjie," and John Haynie, a teaching fellow who later became Austin's trumpet teacher.

Haynie developed into a master pedagogue whose trumpet students are all over the professional world. The same may be said of theory professor Robert Ottman, now known as the author of several harmony and sight-singing textbooks published through numerous editions and used widely across the U.S. Ottman liked to give composition assignments to his theory classes, including Austin's. In 1948 Austin wrote a wind quintet for class, and in 1949 produced a quartet for flute, oboe, bassoon, and trumpet. Later he composed a song. Though he had already been writing arrangements for the jazz and concert bands, these Ottman theory assignments were his first original compositions. He proudly admits that he intentionally violated all the theory rules, using "parallel fifths" and adventuresome chromatics, "all the stuff that would get a red mark."

Wednesday School of Music convocations provided a venue for the earliest performances of these compositions. The ensembles were pickup assemblages of student friends. "That sparked self-initiated composition projects. I decided I liked writing as much as I liked improvising." He had been improvising in his jazz playing, and the spark jumped across the road to these serious composing attempts. He likes to quote Barney Childs, a later composer colleague and kindred spirit in California, who has observed that "improvisation is stand-up music making and composition is sit-down."

Student composer

Austin began formally studying composition, though, only in his senior year. As many other composers and composition pedagogues do, Austin asserts, "You teach yourself using models." This attitude, actually a conviction, is expressed forcefully in the writing of his co-authored text, *Learning to Compose*.[1] Note that the title is not "Teaching Composition" or "How to Compose". He and co-author Clark fully embraced the approach that one learns to compose as an intentional, self-driven process, engaging one's musical curiosity and imagination first through the exploration of musical and other artistic models.

For himself, however, he does acknowledge three master composers as his formal composition teachers. These three distinguished composers were Canadian Violet Archer (at North Texas), Frenchman Darius Milhaud (when he was at Mills College near Berkeley), and American Andrew Imbrie (at UC-Berkeley). Austin would certainly think also of informal mentors, especially John Cage, with whom he had a longtime friendship.

Violet Archer was a visiting professor for two years at North Texas, teaching piano as well as composition. Successful in getting performances of her orchestral works, she also performed in the percussion section of the Montreal Symphony. She had studied piano and composition with Bartok, and once played the xylophone part in Bartok's *Music for Two Pianos and Percussion*. Austin studied with Archer during his senior bachelor's and first-year master's years at North Texas, 1950 to 1952. He recognizes now that "I learned the most from her, at least in terms of craft." She directed him by giving specific compositional assignments, prescribing the medium or instrumentation and suggesting model pieces by master composers. For example, one of his assignments was to reflect his study of Bartok violin duets. Archer would also demonstrate composing in certain ways. "Violet Archer's rigor came from her study with Hindemith, sort of my grandfather composer/teacher."

"It was fortunate, serendipity for her to be there, fresh from Yale, for a couple of years. She was extremely important in the development of my craft. But meanwhile, while studying with her, *sub rosa* I was studying Ives' work, like the *Concord Sonata*. I was also fascinated by the *Lyric Suite* of Alban Berg. I didn't model my pieces after what she was composing." Her legacy to him, instead, was "rigor and the importance of practicing composition." She encouraged fluency. Two early Austin pieces that came out of this study with Archer during this time were his *String Trio*, completed in 1952, and a *Concertino for Trumpet and Chamber Orchestra* modeled on Honegger's *Concertino for Flute, English Horn and Orchestra*.

Though Austin continued studying composition with her during her second year, as he started a master's degree, he never majored in composition, choosing music theory instead for the master's. This may seem peculiar, especially as Austin admits he "wasn't seduced by theory" the way he was with composition. The choice may have been in part because of Ottman's strong influence, but also because of the way Austin, like many of us, discovered the fascination of composing. "Why do you start composing? I think it crept up on me – mostly instrumental music, since I was very active as a trumpet player. I sidled up to it and found I enjoyed it. There were several of us who were fascinated with new sounds and began to study new music."

Austin and three other students would go to a multiple piano room and each play a part of a Bartok string quartet; possibly due to Archer's influence, the library had scores of all six. "We bought scores all the time on our own *Lyric Suite*, Hindemith *Quartet in Eb*."

At the time, there was not a strong interest in current American composers such as Copland, but Austin remembers a string quartet written by fellow student Frank Todd made an impression on him. Todd also played in the top jazz band, and in fact, most of the serious "jazzers" studied composition. Other composition students at North Texas during this time included J.B. Floyd, William F. Lee, Paul Elliott, and Robert Gauldin (who won the very first BMI student composer competition).

It turns out it would be many years later, some six years into Austin's tenure at the University of California at Davis, before he actually taught a composition course himself. Dary John Mizelle and Stanley Lunetta were students in that first seminar. But we're getting ahead of ourselves and will come back to this thread in "California". And we'll also return to the North Texas story in "Later Texas years".

Military and marriage

Graduating again with a Master of Music degree from North Texas State Teachers College in 1952, Austin joined the U.S. Army and became a member of the Fourth Army Band based at Fort Sam Houston in San Antonio. He did arrangements and a little composing in addition to playing trumpet. One project involved assembling a chamber orchestra including string players in the band. He composed *Prosody* for that group. Serving in this group through the summer of 1955 provided many musical opportunities, including performing with personalities. Singer Vic Damone was a member of the unit, and they recorded weekly radio shows.

On a weekend pass, a blind date was arranged with a girl named Olga Navarro. But at the last minute, Olga's steady boyfriend was coming back into town, so Olga asked her sister Edna to take her place. Edna was reluctant to go on a blind date but finally agreed to help her sister. This was an altered blind date that must have gone right, a beautiful young woman and a dashing musician out on the town in romantic San Antonio. And though he was eager to see her again, Edna let him know she was not going to waste her time with a soldier unless he was serious about dating and marriage.

He was. They courted and married in 1953, moved into a tiny garage apartment, and in true fairy-tale fashion, lived happily ever after. By the time Austin left the military in 1955, a family was started with the birth of Don, Jr., then Elizabeth.

California

"One of the reasons I went to California was the Zeitgeist, a West Coast mentality, the avant-garde spirit I eventually expressed in *Source* magazine." Paradoxically, musicology was the other factor that brought Austin to California, for graduate study in that oldest and most respected of scholarly music disciplines at the venerated University of California. Though he had earned the Master of Music degree at North Texas before joining the U.S. Army, he saw a Ph.D. as a stronger credential. When he got out of the Army in 1955, Austin was burned out on bands. His intention in going to Berkeley was to study with American composer Roger Sessions at The University of California and also with acclaimed French composer Darius Milhaud at nearby Mills College. He had reviewed Sessions' harmonic practice book for Ottman's pedagogy course at North Texas. But musicology was also an established discipline and, at UC-Berkeley, a prestigious degree centered around the highly respected musicologist Manfred Bukofzer. James Berdahl was also there as director of bands and by chance heard Austin practicing trumpet. Berdahl asked him to be his teaching assistant, serving as assistant marching band director and teaching assistant with the concert band.

Apparently Austin was an experimentalist even as the leader of the marching band. One early fall day when the Cal Marching Band got new uniforms, the weather was still sweltering. He enlisted his wife Edna to cut off the legs of the old uniforms. (They were living in temporary married-student housing.) The famed UC Marching Band appearing in shorts created a sensation that spread throughout the west coast and Pacific Athletic Conference schools.

Eventually he found himself in a doctoral seminar on sonata form with the distinguished musicologist, Edward Lowinsky. There were only two students in the seminar; the other was Ernest Blank. Both were to choose musical works to analyze and research from a musicological standpoint. Austin chose the first movement of Beethoven's *Eroica* and Mozart's Symphony No. 29 in A Major. But instead of carrying out an orthodox investigation, he went about editing and recomposing the Mozart score "to improve it"! He adjusted the architecture [see *Learning to Compose* for a description of Austin's and Clark's concept of musical architecture], and changed proportions of the basic form, shortening or lengthening proportions according to his own compositional impulses. To put it bluntly, Lowinsky was scandalized. Much later Austin again tinkered with Mozart in his 1986 work, *Sinfonia Concertante: A Mozartean Episode*. It was modeled after another famous Mozart work, yet clearly a free and fresh modern fantasy. The use of Mozart's own words from letters, spoken and recorded by a modern actor, makes not a caricature of Mozart but a respectful character study.

Another obvious example of modeling a new composition on an older one is his *Variations...beyond Pierrot*, using the same instrumentation of Schoenberg's landmark work and exploring its ethos with new sounds and expressions. From the Berkeley musicology years to the present, Austin sees no gulf separating the old and the new, only a rich continuum of many musical ideas and possibilities.

Student composer again

While in Berkeley studying musicology, composition was still luring him. The opportunity to study with the great Darius Milhaud at nearby Mills College was another intersecting path in his journey to become mainly and, eventually, exclusively a composer. "I would say Milhaud had the most influence on me at a critical time as I was an emerging professional. I chose him knowing I was going to Berkeley with Mills nearby. And knowing his work with jazz, like other French musicians. I was also curious about Brubeck." He would attribute the most influence to Milhaud, though his study with the French composer was only for six weeks. But it was a very intense six weeks, with a master class each day for a small seminar, held around the piano in the living room of Milhaud's home. Milhaud was often seen doing his own prolific composing, in ink like Mozart, as students would arrive.

The first day, Milhaud asked Austin what he wanted to work on. Austin said a string quartet. The second day, he had three pages of sketches done, with a form diagram in classic form structure at the top of the first sketch page. "I put the manuscript on the piano rack. He was fixated on the diagram. 'What is zis, Misseur Austin?' I explained it was my plan. He said, 'How can you know what you're going to do until you do it?' And he wrote a big 'X' across my diagram."

Austin remembers the female students in Milhaud's master class all modeling their compositions so closely on the master's that they became, in his disdainful view, "*petites Milhauds.*" But this was imitation, not the deeper digestion and creative response Austin would pursue in his later works. And throughout his later homages to Mozart, Schoenberg, Debussy, and certainly Ives, Austin never composed anything based directly on Milhaud's work, though he admired it immensely. (At North Texas, Austin had not remembered there being any female composition students. He does remember that Copland had already written the book, *What to Listen for in Music*, in which he renounced any female ability in composition. But by the time of *Source* magazine, women composers were seeking out opportunities. He was eager and pleased to include them in

Source. And the first subscriber was none other than Darius Milhaud.)

The next to last day of the Milhaud seminar was a concert for finished works. Austin had completed the first movement of the string quartet. His wife Edna came to the concert, pregnant and holding son Don. At intermission or after the end of the concert, Milhaud, in his wheelchair, called Edna to him. "You're Larry Austin's wife. Your husband will go far." Many years later, as Austin was preparing for his own 2005 master class residency at the Atlantic Center for the Arts, he expressed the intention to re-enact the intensity and impact of the Milhaud master classes.

The day after the concert, at the final seminar gathering, Milhaud expressed the desire to hear some jazz. When he asked each student if they played jazz, only Austin said yes. Milhaud observed, "It doesn't come out in your music!" Austin's next piece, *Homecoming*, was his first jazz piece. While writing it, he began studying with Andrew Imbrie at UC-Berkeley for what would turn out to be a three-year period.

Austin notes that Imbrie was not as prolific a composer as either Archer or Milhaud. Imbrie once said to him, "I don't understand in a jazz composition, with 32-bar 'variations,' why at the last minute there'll be a change to a new key, instead of going back to the original key." His first project for Imbrie was a mass for chorus and orchestra, a traditional form and medium. But the tonal language was not to the teacher's liking. Imbrie was playing the opening of the *Kyrie* at the piano; the harmonies were frustrating him. Imbrie struck the chords over and over again, saying, "You really like ugly chords, don't you?"

In the spring of 1958 the University of California - Berkeley concert band went on a tour that included a performance at the University of California - Davis. Austin conducted his own *Fanfare and Procession* composition. He commented much later that "my conducting style was quite enthusiastic," modeled after George Morey at North Texas. UC-Davis professor and music chairman Jerome Rosen spotted him, and had also heard one of Austin's pieces at the San Francisco Composers Forum. He asked Austin, who was in his third year of doctoral study at Berkeley, to interview at Davis. "Those days you didn't have searches as such," Austin explained. "It was all because of circumstances, having put myself in San Francisco."

The University of California at Davis, well known for its program in agriculture, was in the Fifties and Sixties, according to Austin's description, "a farm school with not much distinction in the arts." He went to Davis in 1958 to teach and conduct the concert band and repertory band – still not teaching composition. So – a band director or composer? A music educator or musicological scholar? Where was this career going?

MacDowell Colony, Bernstein

In 1961, Austin enjoyed the first of five residencies at the MacDowell Colony. The Colony, founded in 1907, is the oldest artist colony in the United States. (Austin's other residencies followed in 1962, 1981, 1982, and 1986.) His first studio had a commemorative wooden paddle signed by the playright Thornton Wilder. At the recommendation of Gunther Schuller, who had visited Davis, he planned to write an orchestra piece with jazz influence. BMI gave him a commission, and it was to be premiered by the National Symphony at Schuller's concert series of jazz in the spring of 1962.

When he returned to MacDowell Colony in 1962, he had a reel-to-reel tape recording of the National Symphony performance of *Improvisations*. But he was there to write a new piece, *Broken Consort*. While he was there, Leonard Bernstein showed up for four weeks to write *Chichester Psalms*. Bernstein knew nothing of Austin's music. One day by chance Bernstein offered Austin a ride to Austin's studio in the woods, whereupon he invited himself in, sat down at the piano, and launched into playing Austin's *Piano Variations*, a jazz-influenced 12-tone score Austin had in the studio. Bernstein remarked that MacDowell himself "would turn over in his grave if he knew this kind of music was being written here."

It happened that they left the Colony the same day in Bernstein's car, going together to the New Haven train station. Whereupon Bernstein asked for a copy of *Improvisations*, the Schuller/BMI piece. Austin promptly produced a score from his briefcase, and Bernstein asked for the tape as well. Shortly after this took place, Bernstein wired from Monte Carlo, "HAVE OPEN SLOT AT END OF SEASON STOP CAN YOU TAKE OUT THE VIOLINS STOP". Austin eagerly produced a second version obliging this instrumentation request.

The piece was to be on a program with Isaac Stern playing a concerto, but Stern apparently wouldn't stand for it. Instead, Bernstein made a special concert of jazz influences along with music by Schuller and Copland, "Jazz in the Concert Hall". Copland played piano on his own work. After hearing Austin's piece, Copland said, "Congratulations Larry – not my cup of tea," referring to the adulterating of "pure jazz" in a third-stream blending with avant-garde concert music. Parenthetically (or perhaps not), while Austin was in New York for the performance, back at Davis, Rosen and other colleagues were making fun of Bernstein at a party, which Edna Austin attended as a loyal, if uncomfortable, proxy spouse.

Austin could not get away to travel back to New York for a subsequent performance of *Improvisations* on a televised Young People's concert. Later he did, however, send some sketches of his massive *Universe Symphony* project to the Jim Fox agency for consideration on Bernstein's Bicentennial concerts. Bernstein apparently commented only "he's a very nice man" but didn't embrace the work.

Improvisation

A couple of experiences helped launch *Source* magazine, which would in turn launch Austin's full devotion to making and promoting new music as an experimental composer. One was an improvisation ensemble he formed with two students, Stanley Lunetta and Dary John Mizelle. Going back to Austin's Barney Childs quote, this was "stand-up composition" of the liberating sort that Austin the jazz trumpeter was always eager to do.

At Berkeley, the jazz thread of Austin's musical passions had continued with the formation of a free jazz improvisation pickup group. At Davis, the improvisation work became more experimental. Austin was familiar with Lukas Foss's improvisation ensemble in Los Angeles, a group that made set pieces with prescribed elements and forms to structure their improvisation. Austin was interested in, and pursued more totally free, spontaneous improvisation. Thus was born the New Music Ensemble at UC-Davis.

The New Music Ensemble intentionally used no charts, though it did have pieces based on a particular concept. The first gesture played would always be crucial, like a Grundgestalt. Then interactions between individual players would unfold. The group did rehearsal exercises exploring a particular kind of phrase gesture and many of its possible permutations. Different gestural qualities naturally arose out of instrumental characteristics and constraints of breath, bow, percussive materials, etc. And there were vivid personalities stirred into the mix – NME member Stan Lunetta, according to Austin, was "a wild man."

Rome

The other *Source* impetus was a year's residence in Rome, where he was involved in more improvisation and collected scores of new works by Cornelius Cardew, Frederic Rzewski, Roland Kayn, Mario Bertucini, Allen Bryant, Franco Evangelisti, and Aldo Clementi.

The University of California system offered Creative Arts grants, one of which, combined with a sabbatical, gave Austin in 1964-65 the resources and opportunity to travel with his family and work abroad for a year. Wanting to immerse himself and his family in a foreign culture with a great musical tradition, he chose Italy. He knew about the American Academy in Rome, where American composers Bill Smith and John Eaton had created an electronic music studio. They would let him use the studio, which turned out to involve regular gratuities to the concierge to let him into its basement space.

Awarded tenure in 1964 partly for his success as a band director, Austin was also succeeding as an innovative and ambitious composer. Taking the whole family along on his Rome studies was by all recollections a great adventure. It was also a bold step in his advancing self-image as a composer and maker of "cutting-edge" experimental music.

Eaton offered to let the Austin family sublet his old apartment. They drove from the Frankfort airport to Rome, staying overnight in Milan. They arrived in Rome the second night and had to find Eaton to get the key. Finally, exhausted, they went to sleep. But the place turned out to be a seedy former brothel with frightening traffic whizzing by the front doorstep. The adventure ended swiftly, as they soon found a nice flat more suitable to the family's needs. For the Austin children's schooling, Thais (born 1960) and Don (born 1954) went to Italian schools, while David (born 1957) and Elizabeth (born 1955), attended English-speaking Marymount. Aurora (born 1962) was two years old, but as an adult she still remembers some of the wondrous sights and discoveries the family experienced together.

Smith and Eaton asked Austin to write a clarinet and piano duo for them to perform for their Venice Biennale duo concert. The result was *Current*, called an "American action piece" by Italian critics. The concert also included works by Schuller, Smith, and Eaton. Austin also wrote there a string quartet, an orchestra piece, an electronic work called *Roma*, and started *Changes* for trombone and tape. And following his habit from Berkeley and Davis, he instigated an improvisation group, convincing some expatriates and local musicians to form what became known as *il*

Gruppo di Improvisatione de Nuova Consonanza. Founders of the group, which kept going after Austin returned to California, included Cardew, Rzewski, Roland Kayn, Mario Bertucini, Allan Bryant, Aldo Clementi, and Franco Evangelisti, its main organizer.

When he returned to UC-Davis in the fall of 1965 after the tremendously stimulating experiences of Rome, he finally got the chance to teach the composition seminar. There were only two students: again, Stanley Lunetta and Dary John Mizelle. They resumed their improvisation ensemble work, and the "sit-down" composition seminar consisted of brainstorming musical ideas. And they looked at many of the new scores Austin had brought back from Europe. The three decided to start a publishing operation to distribute these European experimental scores, maybe producing a catalog to give away as a promotional item. But many of the scores were just one-page concepts, springboards for improvisation; a catalog excerpt would have meant giving away the whole piece.

Hosting Stockhausen and Cage

In 1966-67 Karlheinz Stockhausen was in residence at Davis as a Regents Professor. He seemed not to be interested in the improvisation work Austin had developed there, but instead was intent on his own fixed compositional processes. But when Stockhausen went back to Cologne, he too created his own improvisation group. David Tudor was at Davis at the same time doing live electronic music. According to Austin, Tudor was actually more influential than Stockhausen on the young composers there.

The other important guest composer invited to visit Davis was John Cage. Thus, it was in Davis that Austin heard a performance of Cage's *Atlas Eclipticalis*. This encounter was to prove the beginning of a long friendship between the two experimentalists, with many other professional and personal encounters. Austin invited Cage in 1972 to Tampa for a concert of Cage's work; Paul Jacobs played *Cheap Imitation*. When Cage was a guest in Denton, Texas, in 1981, he heard Austin's *Canadian Coastlines*, remarking afterwards, "It's beautiful; I don't understand it." Cage was prompted to invite him to compose something for Merce Cunningham's "Coast Zone" choreography, leading to Austin's *Beachcombers*.

SOURCE magazine

"I self analyze; if I find that everyone is doing what I'm doing, I stop doing it." Thus, Larry Austin clearly proclaims his self-view as one of a trendsetter, not a follower. And he lived up to that mandate over the entirety of his career as a composer. (Was he also an experimental marching band director?) Arguably the most influential trend-setting project, and unquestionably the most famous (or infamous, depending on one's bias), was *Source* magazine.[2]

When *Perspectives of New Music* (*PNM*) came out in 1962, it offered great promise as a serious journal, a forum for fresh new thinking about music and its possibilities in contemporary culture. Austin subscribed enthusiastically but was quickly disappointed. He found the writing to be intent on prescribing a compositional orthodoxy. Indeed, one prevailing view of how to legitimize and gain acceptance for the new musical expressions of the Fifties and Sixties was through analysis. The theory was if the music's opaque complexities could be illuminated by rational explanation of methodology, its abstract, intellectual beauty would be grasped and embraced.

But Austin was having none of that. He wanted the embrace but cared not for legitimacy. Though the reaction took five years to incubate, when Austin founded *Source: Music of the Avant Garde* in January of 1967, he intended for it to be the opposite of PNM. Eschewing analytic orthodoxy, he embraced exuberant experiment. Even the title, *Source*, was aimed at the bulls-eye of scholarly orthodoxy. Musicology training at UC-Berkeley had taught him to distinguish primary, secondary, and tertiary sources; titling his journal was his impudent way of asserting the primacy of the creative act.

The Lunetta/Mizelle/Austin project turned into a magazine. From the start, it was "anti-academic". The three composers would select contents not by academic jury process but by their own personal interests. Design of the magazine was of considerable importance. Spiral binding allowed the music to be placed open on a music rack and played. The landscape format of pages added to that convenience. Scores were mostly hand drawn, not engraved, emphasizing that they were original source artifacts. A Davis designer, Hamilton Stevenson, was engaged to ensure the magazine's graphic quality. Six investors put in $200 each: Austin, Mizelle, Lunetta, composer/performer Wayne Johnson, UC-Davis colleague Art Woodbury, and family friend Paul Robert, who became business manager, operating out of his house on University Drive in Davis.

Stevenson designed a brochure announcing a price of $9 for a first-year two-issue subscription. The whole $1200 was spent on making and mailing the brochure. In response, they got 500 subscriptions and spent the entire proceeds on printing 1000 copies of Issue 1. The first article was a conversation between Austin, Karlheinz Stockhausen, and Robert Ashley.

At first the editors solicited scores from selected composers. Eventually scores were submitted unsolicited. Two of these were from Texas composer and performance artist Jerry Hunt, who would reconnect with Austin many years later in Texas, when Austin invited him to be a guest in the Center for Experimental Music and Intermedia Event Series. Eventually they received unsolicited submissions that were too much like pieces they had already included in the first three issues. There was the dreaded imitation again. Their reaction? Issue 4 showed a bonfire on the cover, and though it was a mostly overlooked detail, Issues 1 through 3 were depicted fueling the fire, a dramatic way to express the impossible challenge of never falling into an established profile.

After Issue 1, they started printing 2000 copies of each issue, eventually building to as many as 1600 or 1700 subscribers. Many were libraries. My first glimpse of a *Source* issue was in the upper-floor library of the School of Music building on the University of Michigan's north campus in Ann Arbor. Hungry young student composers and curious professors poured over them together and individually, peering through this window into a brave new musical world.

Now *Source* is a serial piece of art and cultural history, an intriguing graphic record of the Avant Garde. Douglas Kahn, a techno-cultural-studies professor at Davis, and Austin have edited a retrospective re-publication of *Source*, including "secondary source" scholarly writing about it.[3] The current UC-Davis music department chair, Pablo Ortiz, is supportive of the project, and Austin was invited back to campus in April 2003 and asked to reminisce about the Davis music department in the Sixties. Unfortunately, many of his memories are not pleasant.

Two important colleagues during those times were Jerome Rosen and Richard Swift. In 1969 the whole department unanimously opposed Austin for promotion to full professor, because he was "too radical" according to Rosen. Though the negative recommendation was eventually overridden by the chancellor, it left a bitter taste. "My family and I both have scars from the latter years at Davis."

When he left Davis, their oldest daughter Elizabeth was a high school sophomore. The first double issue of *Source* was in the works with John Cage as guest editor. Austin was still directing the concert band and repertory band. When he came on stage to conduct the fall 1970 band concert, there was cold silence, the customary applause finally initiated only by his most loyal fans, the Austin family.

Florida Years

During the 1971-72 year at Davis, Austin was called "out of the blue" by the dean of the College of Fine Arts at University of South Florida in Tampa. Looking for a new music department head with expertise in experimental music, they also sought Robert Ashley and Charles Wuorinen as candidates. As Austin interviewed with the faculty search committee, the dean attended, promptly cancelling the search to move ahead and hire him. It is not clear if Austin realized what an ominous sign this may have been about the state of politics in the department and college.

Accepting the position, Austin moved the family to Tampa. He began in earnest in the summer of 1972, with the clear impression he had a mandate (at least from the dean) for aggressive change in the department. He looked first at "their outmoded curriculum". The music faculty was factionalized; "There was great resistance to my ideas." But he was not one to cave in to resistance and forged ahead.

In the summer of 1972, the dean brought together all the chairs in the college, asking for competitive proposals for a $10,000 project grant. Austin and the new drama chair teamed up and proposed an ambitious interdisciplinary, interdepartmental project which they called "Systems Complex for Studio and Performing Arts". They were awarded the $10,000 grant (a fairly substantial one for 1972) and, amongst other things, bought a DEC computer. They also got new faculty lines for what was to become known as SYCOM.

Meanwhile, back at the music faculty, things were not so positive. There was "a near riot" as 20 or so music faculty stormed into a curriculum committee meeting, protesting Austin's progressive (or as they saw it, radical) agenda for change. It took only six months into his tenure for this backlash to coalesce into a successful move to force him out as chair.

Flash forward: Austin's last three years of academic life were spent serving as chair of the composition division at what was by then the University of North Texas College of Music. For Austin, this responsibility "was a healing process for me, vindicating my abilities to chair a program."

But that gets ahead of the story. He remained at South Florida until 1978, directing and developing SYCOM, where Cort Lippe, now a leading practitioner of computer music, studied with him.

During this period, in the summer of 1976, Austin traveled to Aspen, Colorado, for the performance of one of his pieces at the annual Contemporary Music Festival there. Driving back to Tampa afterwards, he stopped in Denton to see Merrill Ellis, electronic music pioneer and director of the North Texas State University Electronic Music Studio. He had first met Ellis when he returned to Denton in 1968 for a ceremony to be given a Distinguished Alumnus Award at North Texas State. This time, when he dropped in, Ellis said, "the dean wants to talk to you," referring to then Dean Marceau Myers. When he went into the dean's office, Myers asked him how he would design an experimental music laboratory/performance space. With his SYCOM experience and ambitious agenda in mind, Austin readily described a black box with a high ceiling, a light grid, and a cyclorama for multiple projection surfaces.

Another flash forward: that turns out to be precisely the description of what was to become an important concert space at North Texas. The new music building completed in 1978 at North Texas contained a black-box theater with light grid and, eventually, a cyclorama. After Ellis' death, it was named the Merrill Ellis Intermedia Theater in memory of the founder of experimental music there – who apparently, along with the dean, had embraced Austin's ideas.

Later Texas years

By 1977 the school Larry Austin had attended as North Texas State Teachers College had become North Texas State

University. The very large School of Music was continuing to expand, creating new faculty lines in a few music specializations. One was computer music. Merrill Ellis, who had founded the Electronic Music Studio in the Sixties, had the vision to see the need to acquire expertise in this emerging field.

When Austin interviewed, he was already recognized as a leader in the field and had already been designated (in 1968) a Distinguished Alumnus of NTSU. A small irony: during his interview with the composition faculty (Ellis, William Latham, Newell Kay Brown, the author, and coordinator Martin Mailman), the coordinator's studio in Chilton Hall, a converted former dormitory, had been Austin's old dorm room.

In a real sense, he came back home, both to a professional environment in which he could thrive and, especially for his wife Edna, to a cultural home. With grant writing and administrative support, he acquired a series of progressively more sophisticated computer music systems, including a Synclavier II and later a NeXT cube. The black-box theater he had discussed with Ellis previously (and now named the Merrill Ellis Intermedia Theater) was a ready venue to display his experimental works, as well as those of frequent guest artists and Austin's many advanced composition students.

When Ellis died in 1981 and was replaced by composer and multimedia artist Phil Winsor, Austin and Winsor collaborated to establish the Center for Experimental Music and Intermedia. CEMI would continue the Ellis tradition and become a leading center worldwide for computer music and experimental multimedia performance art. Austin masterminded and the author coordinated a CEMI Event Series, featuring a fascinating parade of guest composers and performance artists. The more exotic of the latter included Bart McLean playing the spokes of a bicycle wheel, Jerry Hunt banging on a suitcase, and Ellen Fullman, who installed her "Long String Instrument" in the Intermedia Theater. The instrument consisted of harpsichord wire anchored to opposite walls and stretching 40 feet across the theater, played by Fullman walking the length of the strings stroking them with rosin-coated gloves.

In 1981 Austin directed and hosted the International Computer Music Conference, attracting some 300 participants and featuring luminaries in the field such as Lejaren Hiller and John Cage. It has been said that the 1981 ICMC set the standard for subsequent ICMC events. Austin went on to serve from 1990 to 1994 as President of the International Computer Music Association.

Having collaborated with Clark in the planning and execution of the 1981 ICMC, Austin later proposed jointly authoring a book on composition. Bringing distinct yet compatible compositional views and musical values, the two set to work. Each wrote first drafts of chapters, which would be poured over, debated and edited together over regular, long, working lunches. The result, *Learning to Compose – Modes, Materials and Models of Musical Invention*, published in 1989 by Wm. C. Brown, would represent their joint exploration into the deepest dimensions of their creative art.

CDCM

Always a leader and instigator, Austin founded in 1986 another important organization, the Consortium to Distribute Computer Music, established as a commercial collaboration with Centaur Records. The consortium he created brought together six computer music centers: Bregman Electronic Music Studio, Dartmouth College; Center for Contemporary Music, Mills College; Center for Experimental Music and Intermedia, University of North Texas; Experimental Music Studios and Computer Music Project, University of Illinois; iEAR, Integrated Electronic Arts, Rensselaer Polytechnic Institute; and Winham Laboratory, Princeton University. CDCM (with Austin as president for its first 15 years) has been responsible for the making and sale of some 39 Centaur compact discs of computer music. Featured in the series are many samplers of work at various computer music centers including CEMI, as well as numerous Austin compositions.

International travel and residencies

International travel increased for Austin as well. From the early Eighties through his retirement in 1996 and beyond, he was much sought after as a guest composer, participating in a large number of performances of his new works (most composed at CEMI) around the globe and the nation. This was a period in which he enjoyed performances of major works in Warsaw, Saarbrucken, Berlin, Venice, Stockholm, and The Netherlands. The International Institute for Electroacoustic Music, Bourges (France) awarded Austin the prestigious *Magistère* prize in 1996.

International residencies gave him retreat opportunities to finish works in concentrated sessions away from CEMI. After a residency at the Banff Center for the Arts in British Columbia, in 1994 the Sonology Center at Kunitachi School of Music (near Tokyo) invited him to work in their studios. "I'm a hard worker in residencies, arriving early at the studio, staying late each day." The students at Kunitachi were amazed at his dedication to his work. "I was stimulated, and dove into the culture."

Variations...beyond Pierrot was a natural piece to work on in this environment, a piece using four languages, English, German, French, and Japanese. He recorded a Kabuki actor reciting Pierrot poems in Japanese. The piece turned out also to be a wellspring of material for later projects.

In what would become a biennial pattern, in 1996 he went next to the BEAST studios at the University of Birmingham (UK). There he worked on *Djuro's Tree* and also realized his first ambisonic recordings from pre-existing sonic material, the inception of what would become *Ottuplo, four inter-episodes for real and virtual string quartet.*

In 1998 the Rockefeller Center in Bellagio, Italy, offered a residency in an elegant setting on the shores of Lake Como. He brought his own recordings, and while there, finished the score for *Táragató!* He continued work on *Ottuplo* as "a paper-and-pencil seat-of-the-pants" project.

Two years later, in 2000, he finished *Ottuplo* in the Electroacoustic Music Studios at the University of York (UK). Later that year came a residency at the International Institute for Electroacoustic Music, Bourges (France), 2000, where he worked on *Williams Mix*, collecting sounds and writing initial computer program ideas (later to be completed by Michael Thompson) for manipulation of the I Ching. Bourges is somewhat isolated in French wine country, an excellent place to concentrate on work. Nonetheless, *Williams Mix* was not complete when his visit ended.

In 2005 the Atlantic Center for the Arts hosted Larry Austin as Master Artist in Residence, one of three artists to hold simultaneous three-week seminars for carefully selected student participants. Austin had been recommended by former master artist Robert Ashley and others. The center has a dance studio and well-equipped music studio, including electronics, a library with art books and music scores, and a dining commons. Austin worked on his Mozart *Adagio* while there.

Seventeen people responded to Austin's statement of objectives, applying as associate artists. He chose eight, several of whom had studied with former Austin students Michael Matthews, James Phelps, and Elainie Lillios. Coming from such places as Mexico City, Beijing, Japan, Serbia, and the US (University of Michigan), the associate artists brought an international perspective to a sort of musical summit meeting.

Academic career coda

As the UNT School of Music became a College of Music, the series of professors who served as Division Chair of

Compositions Studies included Austin, in 1993 through 1996. After his frustrating experience in Tampa with academic administering, his successful stint as Division Chair was a personal validation. By the time of his retirement from UNT in 1996, he had left a significant mark on the division, the college, and academic practice in the world of experimental music.

Shortly after retirement and his recognition as Professor Emeritus, Larry and Edna Austin moved to the rural edge of Denton, Texas, to an upscale residential community called Robson Ranch. Self-contained with all needed hardware and software in what he calls "gaLarry," and despite significant medical challenges for himself and his wife Edna, Larry Austin continued to make new pieces on commission and to travel widely. His eightieth birthday was celebrated with a gala concert of his music at UNT-Denton on September 12, 2010.

Larry Austin with family, 1968 photo by David Freund
(appeared in *Source* Issue 4)

LARRY AUSTIN'S WORK

What kind of composer are you?

Larry Austin and John Cage first met in Davis, California, in the early 1960s, when Cage visited along with the Merce Cunningham Dance Company. Thus began a lifelong association and friendship of kindred musical spirits. In 1981 (the year Austin invited Cage to be featured guest composer at the ICMC), Austin visited Cage and Cunningham at their apartment while in New York City. Austin was on his way to the MacDowell Colony to write an opera. Cage prepared a meal, followed by conversation while sharing a scotch whisky. Austin asked the inevitable question one asks of a composer: "If you were asked what kind of composer you are, what would you say?" Cage's simple response, "an experimental composer," was effortless and apt. He embraced the identity on two levels – experimenting with materials and ideas; and experimenting with the act of composing itself. It gave Austin extra validation (if he needed such) for a philosophy and an artistic stance he had already adopted for himself.

Austin likes the thought that Ives' father was an inventor, and so was Cage's father. "I still have the attitude of experiment. In the piece I'm doing, I am excited to be discovering new possibilities, even with techniques I've used extensively." At the time of that observation, 2003, he was referring to the technique of convolution, a computer music technique with which he had experimented and developed as a favored tool of his musical language.

At a SEAMUS conference in San Jose, *Accidents Two* was performed. Composers Bart and Priscilla McLean were in attendance; after the performance they looked astounded. Bart exclaimed, "I never know what to expect from you, Larry!"

At a reception after attending a concert in New York (that included a Lukas Foss premiere), Austin was asked the same question he had asked Cage. His impromptu reply took a different angle: "I'm a composer's composer." Or perhaps that may be saying the same thing – a composer determined to work on the cutting edge experimenting with new possibilities in new ways that other composers might follow and emulate.

Improvisation

Considering the progression of Austin's musical endeavors described in Larry Austin's Life, it is no surprise that his work that first brought national acclaim was titled *Improvisations* (1961). After his early immersion in jazz in Texas, he instigated a series of improvisation groups, exploring beyond jazz idioms, in Berkeley, then Rome, and especially in Davis, California.

The question of how to connect his discoveries in free-form improvisation with the more structured improvisation traditions of jazz was one he gave much thought – he has always referred to *Improvisations* as a "third-stream" piece. Designed to merge, to fuse these two approaches to harmony and form, the piece had the precise experimental intent to see what sparks of energy could arise from the fusion. Commissioned by BMI, it caught Leonard Bernstein's attention in the dawning of an era of explosive change in classical music style. One can see the tumult of that brewing change in Austin's score, which posed some notational challenges in attempting to integrate the contrasting ensembles, a jazz trio and a symphony orchestra.

For the rest of the Sixties, there followed a string of no less than nine Austin works whose titles made clear by including the phrase "open style" that the discoveries of *Improvisations*, merging compositional design with improvisational spontaneity, were shock waves of considerable artistic reverberation. One such piece was *Catharsis: Open Style for Two Improvisation Ensembles* (1965). The score for this piece features instructions written out in English. For example, "All instrumentalists quickly and quietly play a flurry of notes in a 5" time span...", and arrows indicating moments of synchronization.

Homage variations

Emulating or outright quoting of an earlier composer's work has a venerable tradition throughout music history. Austin's earliest musical quotation may have been for his piece, *Walter* (1970), which uses material from Vivaldi. His *Tableaux: Convolutions on a Theme* (2003) draws upon Mussorgsky. *Sinfonia Concertante* (1986) incorporates not only musical gestures but also the orchestration and even the title of a well-known Mozart work. In another convergence of compositional approaches, *Sinfonia Concertante* also utilizes spoken words of Mozart – actually a recording of an actor reading from Mozart's letters. The result is not so much a re-creation of the Mozart work as a magical fantasy fusing Mozartean spirit with modern sounds, gestures, and form.

> "*Sinfonia Concertante: A Mozartean Episode* (1986) is modeled on the dramatic essence of its classic namesake: the interplay of the chamber orchestra and the computer music narrative; of sweet consonance and angry dissonance; of innocence and duplicity; of pleasure and sorrow. Dualities intrigue me, because they are never completely reconciled, just as polarities in the fortunes of life are never completely understood. The text for the taped narrative heard through the piece is formed from excerpts from ten letters written by Mozart from Mannheim and Paris to his father in Salzburg during a nine-month period from November 22, 1777, to July 9, 1778."[4]

The piece turns out to be a slice of history in another way. Austin worked on *Sinfonia Concertante* at MacDowell Colony during his fifth and what turned out to be his last residency there. In 2011 a younger Texas composer working at the colony, Hank Hehmsoth, came across its finished score in the collection. It bears the inscription,

"To MacDowell Colony – with fond memories of where this piece began in 1986. – Larry Austin 8/12/88"

Another Austin score, his mini-opera for bass-baritone and tape, *Catalogo Voce*, is also there at MacDowell, in mint condition with a similar inscription.

With an Austin work such as *Threnos* there is an emotional as well as material connection with the original music. *Threnos*, an elegy for the victims of the September 11, 2001, attacks in the United States, the old piece built into Austin's new work is the famous "Dido's Lament" from the 17th-century opera *Dido and Aeneas* by Henry Purcell.

The lament affect is preserved and respected, even as it is clothed in very modern sonic costume.

Figure 1: *Threnos* excerpt, Sequence #1

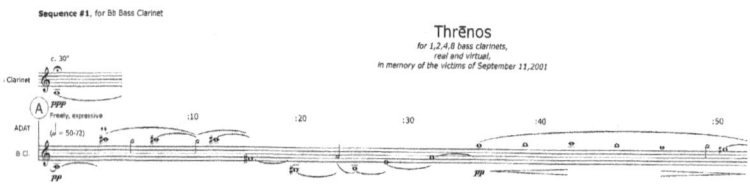

Beyond Pierrot

Variation technique has a long, venerable musical tradition, whether it has been variations on an original theme, variations on a common melody, or variations on a theme by another composer. Famously, Beethoven wrote a set of variations on a theme of Diabelli, Brahms wrote a set of variations on music of Haydn, Rachmaninoff and a host of other composers from Schumann to Lutoslawski composed variations on music of

Paganini, and Stravinsky created variations on music of Pergolesi, or at least a piece that had long been attributed to Pergolesi.

Schoenberg, himself a master of the variations form, was also revered for an early masterpiece, *Pierrot Lunaire*, that was in fact not a set of variations. It was, however, a masterfully lyric, atmospheric setting of expressionist poetry painted in vivid color, elegant lines, and dark sonorities. So much was drawn from a simple ensemble of five instruments (flute, clarinet, violin, cello, piano) and soprano voice that the instrumentation became known by admiring 20th-century composers as a Pierrot ensemble.

So too, Austin has long been fascinated by the work. A commission from Thira, a Canadian ensemble, for their 1994-95 repertoire provided the opportunity to compose *Variations...beyond Pierrot* (1994), a sound-play for soprano, five instruments, hypermedia system, and computer music.

> "The text is taken from the 21 poems Arnold Schoenberg set for his masterwork, 'Pierrot Lunaire', poems originally written by Belgian poet, Albert Giraud, but made famous in German translation by Hartleben, subsequently translated into English and Japanese. The readings I have recorded, processed and combined for the piece range from dramatic to highly stylized. Inspired by but going beyond Schoenberg's musical melodrama, as he described it, my piece is a kind of multi-lingual dream of essences of the poems. In its completed form, the singer will sing, speak, and speak-sing the poems in all four languages, her voice–as well as the five instruments–processed in real-time using MAX and the ISPW."[5]

Austin's treatment, extracting an essence, was to re-create with the same ensemble an open-form work in which the performers improvise on notated gestures drawn from the Schönberg score.

Figure 2: excerpt from piano "moon score" of
Variations...beyond Pierrot

Ives' Universe Symphony

In a 2003 conversation looking back at his career and body of work as a composer, Larry Austin expressed the desire "in the 10 years left in my career" to do an orchestra piece and a string quartet. These are indeed the legacy pieces in a master composer's portfolio. Of the great early-20th-century icons, think of Stravinsky's *Le Sacre du Printemps* and Bartok's six quartets, studied religiously by every educated composer for the rest of the century.

To be sure, Austin by 2003 had already done plenty of both. His first string quartet was in 1955; his 1961 unperformed *Triptych* used string quartet with chorus; and *Quartet in Open*

Style was composed in 1964. The list of Austin compositions employing orchestra is more extensive: chamber orchestra with narrator – *Double Fugue with Prosody* (1954); orchestra and chorus – *Mass* (1958); orchestra and jazz soloists – *Improvisations* (1961); orchestra with piano soloist – *Open Style* (1965); orchestra with narrator, tape and digital synthesizer – *Phantasmagoria* (1977/81); and chamber orchestra with computer-music narrative – *Sinfonia Concertante* (1986). Noticeably absent, however, is a "pure" orchestra piece with no added sound resources... until 1993, with the completion of his realization of Charles Ives' *Universe Symphony*.

Despite the fact that Austin is entirely willing to share the massive work with Ives, it is arguably Austin's (and Ives') *Le Sacre* – or a better comparison, his masterwork for orchestra equivalent to Bartok's monumental late work, *Concerto for Orchestra*. The official title of the work, premiered in 1994, expresses both the compositional provenance and the massive scope of the work:

> *Charles Ives's Universe Symphony (1911-51) as realized and completed (1974-93) by Larry Austin for multiple orchestras, in three continuous sections: PAST–from chaos, formation of the Waters and Mountains PRESENT– Earth and the firmament, evolution in Nature and Humanity FUTURE–Heaven, the rise of all to the Spiritual*

Another preparation was Austin's admiration for Karlheinz Stockhausen's groundbreaking orchestral work of mid-century, *Grüppen*,[6] a piece involving massive, dense contrapuntal textures produced by two orchestras. Its mind-boggling contrapuntal rhythmic complexity meant that every musical line was effectively independent, allowing no perception of any common pulse. The effect of *Grüppen*'s temporal chaos couldn't be more unlike Ives' famous experiments with multiple tempos, or for that matter, Austin's *Canadian Coastlines*.

But both approaches represent diverging branches in the same evolution. As Schoenberg's twelve-tone row was meant to liberate music from tonality, Ives, Stockhausen, Austin and others were liberating it from the tyranny of a single controlling "beat" – ironically, the very ingredient of jazz which Austin the jazz performer methodically transcended through his extensive experiments in free improvisation.

One Austin work, *Maroon Bells* (1976), with its quite literal mountain inspiration, arguably could be ascribed to his affinity with Ives, whose music included mountaintop imagery. Since the early Seventies, when Austin had begun studying Ives' sketches for what he believed was Ives' "most compelling and visionary work," four smaller Austin pieces laid the groundwork, testing his ability and approach (both aesthetic and technical) to realizing Ives' conceptions.

- *First Fantasy on Ives's Universe Symphony: the Earth* (1975) for two brass quintets, narrator, and tape
- *Second Fantasy on Ives's Universe Symphony: the Heavens* (1976) for clarinet, viola, keyboards, percussion, and tape
- *Phantasmagoria: Fantasies on Ives's Universe Symphony* (1977, revised 1981) for orchestra, narrator, digital synthesizer, and tape
- *Life Pulse Prelude* (1974-84) for 20-member percussion orchestra

The tape material notated below indicates a pulse-like rhythmic material. Austin wrote in a 1985 article:

"What I term 'the *Life Pulse Prelude* effect' is: Ives's 'durational counterpoint' plus sound-mass/pulsation-mass/event-mass/rhythm-mass/melody-mass plus the phenomenological synthesis of mesmerizing melodic/rhythmic iterations and an incessant improvisatory catharsis ['incessant myriads', Ives called it]. It works. It does, indeed, seem like the life pulse of the Universe."[16]

Figure 3: excerpt from page 7 of *Second Fantasy*

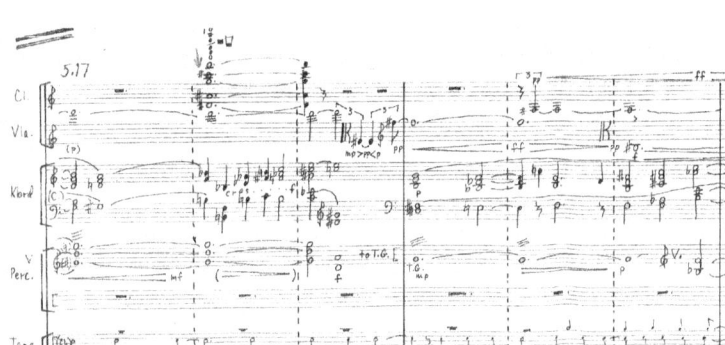

Austin credits the American Academy and National Institute of Arts and Letters, the Charles Ives Society, Inc., and the Yale University Music Library for their support in allowing access to materials for the extensive research he conducted, and ultimately for the permission to publish and record the *Universe Symphony* realization. Ultimately, it is an Ives/Austin collaboration. In Austin's words:

"There are 36 extant sketch pages which I believe are definitely part of the *Universe Symphony*, including completed music, musical sketches and fragments, and detailed narrative and graphic descriptions concerning the form, continuity, and transcendental aesthetic of the work. I began in 1974 to transcribe the musical material and to study Ives's plan for the *Universe Symphony* from reproductions of the extant unpublished manuscripts in the Charles Ives Archives of the Music Library of Yale University. I was inspired not only by the rich musical material found in the sketches for the *Universe Symphony* and by Ives's open invitation to other composers in his Memos to expand on and even to carry out his aspirations for the work: '...in case I don't get to finishing this, somebody might like to try to work out the idea...'

"Four types of compositional material are found in Ives's sketches for his *Universe Symphony:* 1) virtually complete scoring (except for details of orchestration, dynamics, articulation, and phrasing); 2) incomplete scoring; 3) virtually complete formal, structural, and aesthetic descriptions of the nature and technical specifications; and 4) brief and often fragmentary musical and textual sketches exemplifying particular aspects or techniques that Ives was conceiving for the work. My intent in transcribing and interpreting Ives's sketches has been to realize and complete both Ives's explicit and implicit compositional, formal, and aesthetic intent for the work. Hence, to the extent intended and possible, I have meant this realization and completion of Ives's *Universe Symphony* to be experienced and appreciated in performance as a 100% Ives composition."[7]

The 37-minute work, recorded on the Centaur label (1994), if not yet considered a masterpiece, is a powerful demonstration of orchestral potential, of Austin's craft and ingenuity. It is also a masterful expression of Ives' conception, of American music in the 20th century, and of modern or perhaps post-modern art.

Remixing Cage

For Austin to finish the massive work Ives sketched is a task of great devotion. So too was the task of preserving, restoring, and extending another composer's piece. Austin has long been devoted to John Cage as a friend and mentor. Consider the 70th birthday gift composition, *...art is self-alteration is Cage is...* just one of many tokens of the esteem and affection Austin holds for the iconic fellow experimental composer and his provocative work.

Cage's work, *Williams Mix* (1953), is considered seminal in a number of ways. In his chapter on *Williams Mix* for the book, *A Handbook to Twentieth-Century Musical Sketches*, Austin describes its importance: " . . . the legendary primacy of *Williams Mix* as the first octophonic piece in the history of electronic music and the first important work in the genre by the great American composer of experimental music, John Cage."[8] Its significance is even broader, written during an intense period of the early 1950s in which Cage made some of his most influential breakthrough pieces: *String Quartet in Four Parts*, *Concerto for Prepared Piano and Chamber Orchestra*, *Music of Changes*, and *Imaginary Landscape No. 4* (the famous piece for 12 radios).

Not only an early piece of tape music in the *Musique concrète* stream of work, *Williams Mix* was a process piece – algorithmic, employing the *I Ching* and coin-toss chance operations that became a hallmark of virtually all his later work. Cage described his 192-page score (time graph) for the electronic work as a "dressmaker's pattern" for splicing taped segments of various sounds.

The piece required a major collaboration of technicians and other musicians, including David Tudor and the composer Earle Brown. (This was also a significant period for Brown, whose seminal work, *Folio and Four Systems*, was composed in 1952-53.) Cage described the two-person tape splicing process:

> "Earle Brown and I spent several months splicing magnetic tape together. We sat on opposite sides of the same table. Each of us had a pattern of splicing to be done, the measurements to be made, etc. Since we were working on tapes that were later to be synchronized, we checked our measurements every now and then against each other. We invariably discovered errors in each other's measurements. At first each of us thought the other was being careless. When the whole situation became somewhat exasperating, . . . we decided that one person should do all the final synchronizing splices."[10]

When Cage was unable to secure support to establish a center for experimental music, the collaborative project was cut short. Cage's full plan for the 20-minute work was never completed, with only the 4:15 Part I presented in its historic premiere at the University of Illinois in 1953.

Like Ives for the *Universe Symphony* sketches, though, Cage issued an invitation in 1985, stating that "someone else could follow the recipe / with other [sound] sources than I had to make another mix."[11] Austin decided to do just that. After Cage's death, in 1998 he obtained from the John Cage Trust a copy of the score, sketches, and digital audio copies of the eight reel-to-reel tapes. Thus began an intensive, laborious process not just of restoration, but of transformation to a digital realm. This entailed converting Cage's *I Ching* operations to a computer-programmed algorithm and perfecting the timing synchronization of the eight channels of sound to the precision Cage had specified in the score.

Having this algorithmic program, Austin was inspired to compose further while remaining faithful to the expressed spirit of the process Cage had described. He developed a huge library of digital sound files analogous to Cage's tape segments, using the same six categories – city sounds (Tokyo, London, Rome, Bourges, Paris, New York); country sounds (birds, bees, rainforest, livestock); electronic sounds (from Austin's other electro-acoustic pieces); manual sounds; wind sounds; and small sounds. This library enabled him not just to "re-fill" Cage's score but to regenerate it, the programmed algorithmically generated sequences filled with sounds of his own choosing. Austin was understandably pleased with the result:

> "For this composer's heart . . . every run of the Williams [re]Mix[er] brings me a new, stimulatingly joyful, spatial collage of these sounds from my personal library . . . the kind of joy Cage experienced when he heard the first complete performance of *Williams Mix*."[12]

Mapping, Fractals

As with so many American composers of the 20th century, Austin looks to Charles Ives as an iconic pioneer of musical experimentalism. In the 1970s, Austin began a study of the sketches and manuscripts of Ives' unfinished work, *Universe Symphony*. Some of Ives' sketches involve tracings of the outline contours of rock formations. In 1976, at the Aspen Contemporary Music Festival for a performance of his *First Fantasy on Ives' Universe Symphony*, Austin felt it natural and compelling to try out Ives' technique on the majestic Rocky Mountain scenery and cloud formations surrounding him. The pitch contours of strands of synthesized sound were composed to mirror metaphorically those visual shapes. His first mapping piece, *Maroon Bells*, was the result.

Shortly after, Austin began to read Benoit Mandelbrot's first book, in which he reveals the underlying mathematics of such seemingly gently random patterns as cloud shapes, shorelines, and mountain ridges. Mandelbrot called these fractal series. Austin's next mapping piece, *Stars*, created note patterns computer-generated by employing fractal functions to filter a random string of numbers. The next work, *Protoforms*, used the same process.

But Austin did not abandon the technique of mapping actual patterns of nature. In 1980, CBC radio gave an award within its system to do an innovative project. David Jaeger, CBC producer of the "Two New Hours" series, knew of a new music program Austin had been doing for KPFA, Berkeley's public radio station. Jaeger invited Austin to do a "radiophonic" piece, an experimental work to engage the medium of radio in an experimental way. Austin chose to experiment with time, making what he has described as "the ultimate click-track piece". It would be a massively contrapuntal texture, with many instruments playing continuous, independent lines, all in different, independent tempos. The contours of each contrapuntal part were determined using maps of Canadian coastlines, honoring the project's sponsor. Each player's special tempo would be set by a machine-generated click-track played in that individual's headphone. The final layer of experiment was audacious: three separate subsets of the ensemble would perform together for live broadcast, but in three different cities! Players in Winnipeg and Halifax were to have their sounds transmitted to Toronto to be mixed together electronically and the master signal broadcast back out on CBC radio. CBC engineers had gone out on strike the day before the 1981 premiere broadcast, but were given a special exemption to work this event. Austin was on stage in Winnipeg, interviewed before the piece began. "I was frightened to death that something would break down." It did work, however; his notes describe the successful result.

> "Four voices of an eight-voice canon are performed by eight musicians, the remaining four–'the computer band'–played as digital synthesizer sequences pre-recorded on tape,

each voice entering in turn in exact melodic/rhythmic imitation. However, none of the eight voices are performed in the same tempo. Instead, the musicians follow four distinct tempo click tracks, allowing different, concurrent tempos as well as gradually accelerating and decelerating tempos over relatively long spans of time. The click tracks are timed so that the eight voices come into melodic/rhythmic unison—phase five times during the piece; i.e., the voices momentarily catch up with one another, only the next moment to continue the acceleration or deceleration, as the case may be.

"Fractal is a mathematical term coined by French mathematician Benoit Mandelbrot, used to describe a class of natural distribution phenomena involving the spectral density of a fluctuating quantity and its correlation. In the present piece, such fluctuating quantities are derived from freely concatenated mappings of Canadian coastlines, whose courses form coordinates on a graph and provide data for a compositional algorithm generating melodic contour, interval choice, textural density, dynamic flux, and rhythmic design: musical canonic fractals."[13]

There is no score, only a set of individual parts, each with a different tempo specified by click track to be played back in each player's headphones. Rhythms are mildly irregular but not angular, with few sharp contrasts of duration. The lines are relatively continuous, a hallmark of Austin's melodic writing, gently meandering around small "coves" and "peninsulas" in shape. Likewise, a characteristic Austin form unfolds: dense, continuous texture without narrative curve, climax, or dramatic interruption.

Figure 4: Sample part from *Canadian Coastlines*

The taped lines were generated with a Synclavier Digital Music System in the computer music facilities of CEMI at the University of North Texas. Thus it was fitting that *Canadian Coastlines* was performed again at the 1981 ICMC in Denton, this time as a concert piece with all players on one stage – but still listening to different click-tracks and playing at different tempos. John Strawn gave a vivid textural description of this second performance in the *Computer Music Journal*:

> "Canadian Coastlines...is an intriguing work for ear and mind . . . The work thins, thickens, cools, and occasionally warms, moves forward and then veers away, joins, separates, soothes and disturbs, and truly allows the listener to enter the process."[14]

And John Cage remarked to Austin afterwards, "It was beautiful, Larry – I don't understand it." It does indeed have a gentle, ineluctable sonic beauty.

More fractals

Beachcombers (1983) and *Sonata Concertante* (1984) both employ fractal functions to sort and filter raw verbal or musical material with programmed numerical algorithms. Though Austin's notes for *Sonata Concertante* make no mention of fractal processes, focusing instead on issues of form, they are the basis for the compositional process generating material for the piano part.

> "Word strings – linguistic forms – have fractal properties; in a line of text, the frequencies of letters of the alphabet and the size of letter-groupings to make words in sequence may seem unpredictable phenomena; yet in a given language and style those features will take on a consistency over large masses of material. ... The process of extracting fractal data from a word string can be automated. CZWALK, a computer program designed by Austin, ... processes a file of word-lines such as the 'Zone' text used in *Sonata Concertante*."[15]

Representing a culmination of Austin's personal and professional connection to John Cage, the 1982-83 season saw both the birthday tribute, ...*art is self-alteration is Cage is*..., and a historic performance of *Beachcombers* by Cage himself.

> "*Beachcombers* was commissioned in 1983 by John Cage and the Merce Cunningham Dance Foundation for performance with the dance work and film *Coast Zone*, choreographed by Merce Cunningham. The premiere performance by the Merce Cunningham Dance Company took place at the New York City Center Theater on March 18, 1983, performed by John Cage, chanting; David Tudor, electronics; Martin Kalve, cheng; and Takehisa Kosugi, violin. *Beachcombers* is dedicated to John Cage and Merce Cunningham."[16]

Austin's notes for *Beachcombers* allude to both the spatial metaphor of a coastline and a rigorous exploration of a Mandelbrot fractal function.

> "*Beachcombers* are waves and wanderers. Waves rise, fall, crash, thunder, leaving droplet sheets and turbulent eddies. Wanderers explore, close by the waves, up and down the coast zone, walking slower, faster, slower... shifting, changing, searching. . . . The sound image of the surf and the undulating motion of the water are heard both from the tape part and the signal source provided for an envelope follower controlling the shaping of white-noise envelopes. The computer music on tape ∕ is mixed freely during the performance with the amplified instruments/voices: the dodecaphonic wave-patterns derive from a self-avoiding random walk through complete and segmented sentences written by mathematician Benoit Mandelbrot, applying the 'Zipf law of word frequencies'."[17]

Other models

Mapping algorithms and fractal functions are in essence mathematical/scientific processes and functions. Other kinds of starting models for Austin's compositional process include those with a more musical starting point: the work of older composers and the personalities of various contemporaries.

In the latter category, the personality is sometimes named or hinted at in the composition title, such as *Walter* (violist Walter Trampler), *LaBarbara* (singer Joan LaBarbara), or a piece for Dianne Mizelle's bass quartet, Profundis, *...art is self alteration is Cage is...*, The exotic, specially notated score for multiple double basses was written as a 70th birthday gift to John Cage. (Austin reports that Cage sent a note saying, "Thank you. I feel changed already.")

"The score for ...*art is self-alteration is Cage is...* is what I call a *uni-word omniostic*, where all possible arrangements of the letters of one word–here, C A G E–appear adjacently, allowing one to spell the word, continually in sequence, following appropriate horizontal, vertical, and diagonal paths through the array of the word's letters (see score reproduction). The piece was composed between December, 1982, and January, 1983, and "dedicated to my friend and mentor, John Cage, in his seventieth year." The title of the work was inspired by John's definition of art: "Art is self-alteration."

"The performers trace a path through the *omniostic* score, playing each note associated with a letter without expression–but not mechanically–quietly changing to the next note when "...self-alteration is Cage is art is...". Each of the sixty-four block letters–sixteen iterations of C A G E– contains a combination of four pitches and/or silences derived by algorithmic program.

"The score may be played by four string basses, by four 'celli, by quartet combinations of 'celli and basses, or by quartet multiples of such groups. In this recording, four string bass quartets are heard. Notated pitches are limited to the open strings and the first three natural harmonics on each string, the resultant gamut of pitches totaling sixteen. The four strings of each of the four instruments are tuned, *scordatura*, to the pitches c, a, g, and e, each instrument tuned to a different combination of the letters."[18]

FIGURE 5: ...*art is self-alteration is Cage is...* detail

    The harmonies sounded by ambient counterpoint will all consist of only the pitch classes C, A, G, and E, created by scordatura open strings and harmonics. And the open-ended improvisational nature of the work, expressed by an artistically drawn matrix score, is an obvious and elegant homage to Cage's deep interest in chance and open form.

Computer Music

When Larry Austin spent the 1964-65 year in Rome, on leave from UC-Davis, he was allowed to work at the American Academy in an electronic studio set up by William O. Smith and John Eaton. Back at UC-Davis, he acquired equipment and set up his own studio centered around Buchla and Moog analog synthesizers. But his first real opportunity to delve seriously into computer music came in 1968 at Stanford, in a computer music workshop led by John Chowning, Max Mathews, Leland Smith, and James Tenney. Austin's fellow students included David Wessell and Suzanne Ciani.

The Stanford system consisted of MUSIC-5 synthesis software running on an IBM-360 mainframe computer. The software required design of a virtual orchestra and virtual score (note list) in FORTRAN language. And the IBM-360 required use of JCL, Job Control Language. "I hated that," Austin complained. Input was by IBM punch cards; output was to digital tape. For conversion of these digital tapes to analog audio signals on magnetic tape, direct memory access to a Digital PDP-10 was necessary for sufficient speed to convert. All in all, it was an extremely cumbersome and frustrating process; but the results were magical – exotic new sounds no one had heard before, under dramatically more precise control.

Austin had just done *Accidents* a year earlier, and wanted to explore random functions he knew the 360 and FORTRAN were capable of producing (though the system was not ready for his idea to randomly change the digital sampling rate). He did manage to generate material he took back to Davis and finished with the Buchla synthesizer for his piece *Caritas*.

In 1972, now at University of South Florida, Austin and the drama department chair teamed up and proposed an ambitious interdisciplinary, interdepartmental project, which they called "Systems Complex for Studio and Performing Arts". They were awarded the $10,000 grant and, amongst other things, bought a DEC computer. They also got three new faculty lines for what was to become known as SYCOM. In 1976, Austin's USF student Cort Lippe started working with a DEC PDP11-10 mini-computer.

During this time, Austin participated in the first Music Computation Conferences, at Michigan State University in 1974 and University of Illinois in 1975. In 1976, Barry Vercoe was the host at MIT, changing the name to the International Computer Music Conference (ICMC). The ISCM Days were meeting in Boston during the American Bicentennial. Austin did not attend at San Diego in 1977, but did go to Northwestern for the 1978 ICMC. At that meeting, Curtis Roads, Thom Blum, John Strawn and others began organizing what became, by 1980, the Computer Music Association. It couldn't be called an "International" association – something to do with the California Department of State and incorporation rules. It was only in 1990, while Austin was president, that the California Secretary of State approved a request to change the name to ICMA. Finally the association name paralleled the name of the annual international conferences.

In 1980 at the Queen's College ICMC, Austin announced to fellow members an invitation for what was then North Texas State University to host the 1981 conference in Denton. Austin had arrived at North Texas in 1978 from Tampa, filling a new position with a mandate to develop computer music. Through enterprising grantsmanship, he acquired a series of hardware systems, including a Hewlett Packard machine, an MSCI-8080, a Synclavier II, and eventually a NeXT cube. The NeXT machine brought him back to software synthesis, now running MUSIC-5's descendent, MUSIC-360, and eventually CSound.

The 1981 ICMC in Denton was by all accounts a huge success. A grand highlight was a four-hour performance by some seven harpsichordists of *HPSCHD* supervised by the composers, Lejaren Hiller and John Cage. Barry Truax said the 1981 ICMC in Denton was a new model for ICMC organization. It seemed pivotal in engaging international practitioners such as James Dashow, who hosted the 1982 ICMC in Venice. Austin has remarked, "I still feel that the strength of the ICMC, more than just the music, was the papers, especially as they became published in *Proceedings*."

In the early days of electronic music, a "tape piece" was as common a medium for experimental composers as a string quartet had been for conventional composers. Morton Subotnick popularized the "solo" tape piece with works commissioned by Nonesuch Records for LP publication. Austin's electronic music included seven solo tape pieces prior to 1980, including *Caritas* (1969) and *Phoenix* (1974).

Austin has composed virtually all of his most recent pieces using computer music in some way. Many uses, however, have involved sampling "real sounds" for re-synthesis to combine in performance with live singer or instrumentalist – a digital update to the so-called "tape-plus" genre. Fewer of his computer music works are for digital sound to stand alone. One "pure" computer music work, **Stars* (1982), stands out, as it consists entirely of digitally synthesized sounds.

> "The idea for composing **Stars* grew out of my fascination with the symbolic patterning by the ancients of eighty of the eighty-eight constellations seen in the Northern and Southern heavens. I devised a system to derive melodic sequences and unique timbral qualities from each constellation, combined in a composition to form the "future" music tape and digital synthesizer section of my orchestral work, *Phantasmagoria* (1974-81). It was the un-patterned constellations, as well as the total number of stars visible to our eyes–1,917 was my count!–that continued to intrigue me. In **Stars*, exactly 1,917 unique "star-timbres" illuminate a continuously evolving "star-drone" to create my fanciful and, I feel, musical heavens.
>
> "While each star-timbre had its distinct set of random values controlling the frequency modulation ramps,

49

amplitude and side-band functions, all had in common either of two fm indices. The total duration of each star-timbre (from initiation to disappearance) ranged from as brief as a millisecond to as long as a few seconds, these events also controlled by random selection. Such zero-order stochastic process was carefully skewed, however, by continual and very gradual time-unit fluctuations, slowing and accelerating the "beat" over relatively long time spans and creating what the composer feels are intriguing musical coherences.

*Stars, then, is computer music in both the way its compositional elements are formed and in its digital synthesis: in the first instance, the tempo-skewing of randomly generated parameters of the star-timbres, and, in the second instance, the control of the digital sound output of the Synclavier II digital music system."[19]

Since converting to digital technology, several important Austin works have concentrated exclusively on the capability of digital music systems to input digital samples, recordings of speech or environmental sounds (manmade or natural), and then to process, manipulate, and edit sounds into a computer music narrative or soundscape. The starting sound files for ¡Rompido! (1993) were recordings of the Texas sculptor Jesus Moroles cutting granite.

"¡Rompido! means torn!, rent! Its title was inspired by actually seeing and hearing a large piece of granite torn in half...a beautiful sound...a violent act. This music I have composed for dance and granite sculpture combines live performance (optional) on the sculpture by a percussionist with computer-processed chunks of sounding granite heard from the pre-composed digital audio tape. All the sounds and combinations of sounds heard on the tape come from recordings made at exhibits of granite sculpture by Texas sculptor Jesus Bautista Moroles and at his Rockport, Texas, studio or "factory", as he sometimes calls it. In fact, the piece is formed in three continuous scenes, each a sound-montage chronicle from my three field trips to record the chipping, wedging, polishing, sawing, drilling, and tearing of granite."[20]

For *Shin-Edo: CityscapeSet* (1996) recordings of street sounds are sonic postcards from Austin's visit to Japan for a composing residency.

"Inspired by the dynamic sound-scape and culture of Tokyo that I have experienced each day, I explored and recorded those places and sounds that have so heightened my sonic acuity. It is this sonic impression–by a fascinated foreigner– that I want to make into a piece about what I call this 'Shin-Edo', this 'new-inlet'."[21]

For *SoundPoemSet* (1991) and *John Explains* (2007) the raw material was recorded conversations, another stream of compositional interest for Austin to be discussed later. For *Djuro's Tree* (1997) the sources are both environmental sounds and the human voice.

"*Djuro's Tree* is a family portrait of three generations of Serbian mathematicians: Alexandra Kurepa, her father Svetozar and her great uncle Djuro (1907-1993). Alexandra speaks of Djuro's influence on her and her father's careers as mathematicians. Her son Andre tells of his fun at the Adriatic coast every summer. Djuro's family story is set in a dynamically moving octophonic "family" tree of sound, the wind moving through it, the sonic leaves and creaking limbs dramatically animating its soundscape.

"Alexandra Kurepa's narrative and her son Andre's story–in both Serbian and English–were recorded by the composer at their home in North Carolina. The sounds of a tree's limbs creaking and its foliage rustling in a strong wind was taken from the BBC Sound Effects Library. The creaking limbs were "helped" by the recording of a squeaking wooden chair from the Jonty Harrison family kitchen in Edgbaston, England. All the sonic materials for the piece derive from these three sources. *Djuro's Tree* was commissioned by Borik Press."[22]

Thus one of the earliest modes of electronic music composition, *Musique concrète*, comes full circle into the digital world.

Convolutions

The "instrument plus tape" genre has been a staple of electronic music since the earliest analog synthesis tape music of the late 1950s. The tape part could function as an accompaniment; or it could provide the dramatic tension of a "Man vs. Machine" interaction.

As many composers of the second half of the 20th century, Austin was fascinated with and strongly influenced by the music of Varese. In 1998 he wrote to the publisher-owner of Varese's *Octandre*, seeking permission to do a new work based on *Octandre*. Boosey & Hawkes refused permission and threatened legal action. That refusal spawned his approach for the *Redux* series of compositions. The core technique of the approach was what he called a "convolution," both a compositional and a technological technique. As a technological process, two signals are created and interact; one serves as a filter acting upon the other. Compositionally it is a bit like counterpoint in which one musical line is a principal "voice" or melody while a subordinate countermelody or bass line gives harmonic color and inflection. Technically, it is somewhat like AM and FM radio, where a fixed, super-audio carrier signal is modulated by rapid increases to the signal's strength or amplitude (AM) or by rapid increases and decreases in its core frequency (FM). There is a carrier signal and a modulating signal. In Austin's technique, both signals are likely to be recordings of the featured instrument playing passages from the older music. But the two are combined not as a duet but as carrier and modulator. The result is ethereal, producing a ghost-like echo or shadow of the original music. Thus, for example, in *Redux 1* (written for violinist Pat Strange), *Redux 2* (for pianist Joseph Kubera) and *Redux 3* (for clarinetists F. Gerald Errante and D. Gause) recorded computer music becomes a mirror-like environment of sounds in which the same instrument that was a recorded source is also heard "live" as a focal statement of homogeneous thematic material.

> "*Redux* (2007) re-visits and transforms my own violin music from the 'seventies, 'eighties, and 'nineties via both the computer music convolution process and the exemplary playing/recording of sequences from these pieces by violinist Patricia Strange, for whom the piece is composed. *Redux* is the fifth in a current series of pieces for virtuoso performers and octophonic computer music, which I have composed since 2001. But *Redux* will be different from the previous pieces, in that it "plays" on my own previously composed music, rather than varying other "previous" composers' musics, including Purcell, Moussorgsky, Mozart, and Debussy, to be specific. For the technically oriented, the soloist's sounds are amplified, processed, and diffused in the listening space, combined with the synchronized playback of convolved, octophonic computer

music heard in montage: the listener is surrounded and immersed in the live and recorded sounds."[23]

In later work, emerging sound diffusion technology enabled Austin's fascination with spatial aspects of acoustic environments to be explored in a digital realm. In the early days of tape music, spatialization was accomplished by recording four synchronized tracks of sound to be played back by loudspeakers in four corners of a hall. Digital advancements led to the octophonic medium, digital generation of eight synchronized tracks of audio. Instead of laborious creation of taped panning effects (sound in speaker L fades at the same time as same sound emerges in speaker R, perceived as though the sound "moved"), a digital octophonic system enables more complex spatial illusions of sound emanation. Combined with digital control of artificial reverberation and even Doppler pitch effects, a wide variety of virtual rooms can be created in which sounds swirl in a sonic choreography.

Ambisonics

Octophonics enabled Austin to digitally place by compositional/algorithmic design the apparent emanation of sound. Ambisonics, by contrast, involved microphone technology to capture and preserve surrounding sounds in an acoustical setting.

Commissioned in 1998 by the London-based Smith Quartet, *Ottuplo* (2000) was groundbreaking in terms of using this technology to create through ambisonic recording a virtual string quartet. Program notes explain the inception of the work.

"In summer, 1998, Austin was awarded a composer residency at the Rockefeller Center at Bellagio, Italy, to create the written score for the piece–hence, its inspiration from the resounding church bells, thunderstorms, and lake sounds of beautiful Bellagio, heard from Studio Musica in Villa Serbelloni in the village of Bellagio from the promontory overlooking Lake Como. In winter, 2000, Austin was invited for a residency at [University of] York, [UK,] as a visiting research fellow working with the extensive ambisonic research resources of the Electroacoustic Music Studio there."[24]

Figure 6: *Ottuplo* score excerpt

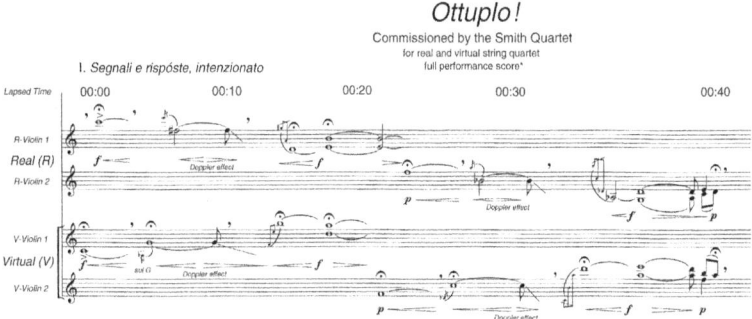

The resulting ambisonic sound environment, an Austin trademark, is a counterpoint between a live, real string quartet and a virtual one. The virtual four strings seem to be surrounding the audience, in the same sense that environmental sounds of church bells, lake, etc., surrounded the composer at the villa.

Conversations

Another John Cage compositional fascination shared by Austin is the use of speech as basic sound material. A direct form of this modeling source can be seen in a work such as *SoundPoemSet*.

Recordings of Austin's individual conversations with Pauline Oliveros, Jerry Hunt, Morton Subotnick, and David Tudor become the raw sonic material for processing, vocal timbre and speech cadence while transforming words and meaning into abstract sound textures.

> "Each *SoundPoem* maps its musical form from poetry created from select aphorisms uttered spontaneously during each conversation. Aphoristic utterances were extracted, analyzed, transformed and synthesized with 'spectral modeling synthesis' (SMS), a sound analysis synthesis technique based on 'deterministic plus stochastic decomposition,' developed at CCRMA by Xavier Serra and Julius Smith."[25]

The process could be thought of as like Cubist portrait painting, though with considerably more profound detachment from the original.

This compositional thread traces back to a 1979 work involving the human voice. John Large, a voice-teacher colleague of Austin at North Texas, was an expert in the mechanism of the voice. Large's commission of a work from Austin resulted in *Catalogo Voce*, a multimedia "mini-opera" in which the voice is accompanied by electroacoustic sounds derived from recorded voice, edited and transformed to emphasize fundamental phonetic elements in abstract sonic textures.

The John Cage influence in Austin's use of speech sounds is most direct in *Beachcombers* (1983). Cage had given a lecture on anarchy at the 1981 ICMC Austin hosted in Denton. Cage called in 1982 to commission an Austin piece for Merce Cunningham's choreography entitled "Coast Zone".

Here two Austin compositional threads converge. At that time he was ardently studying Mandelbrot's writing on fractals. In an ironic twist, Austin applied fractal functions to filter words of Mandelbrot's text on fractals. The irony, however, ended up somewhat hidden. Cage asked if the excerpted phrases of

Mandelbrot's words would have syntax. When Austin answered yes, Cage (who was to recite the words in performance) asked him to remove the syntax, advising that syntax caused audiences to pay too much attention to the words as opposed to just their sonic, musical qualities. Austin responded by deciding to put single words on cards that Cage could shuffle when reading in live performance with the dance.

Austin returned to Stanford in 1989, working on a commission from Pacifica Foundation with Meet the Composer for a work to be broadcast on Berkeley radio station KPFA. Austin describes this work at CCRMA:

> "SANSY: Sound Analysis System, a specialized analysis/ resynthesis/ transformation program written for the Symbolics LISP machine, was developed at Stanford's Center for Computer Research in Music and Acoustics by Dr. Xavier Serra. As this experimental system was being perfected and tested in 1989, I was invited by CCRMA Director John Chowning and Serra to explore SANSY in the creation of *Transmission Two: The Great Excursion* during my composer residency there from May to July and again in December of 1989. As such, *TT:TGE* is the first piece created with SANSY. What I believe to be the unique sonic and musical results 'speak for themselves' through the piece."[26]

Adding recorded conversations with Robert Ashley, Jerry Hunt, Pauline Oliveros, Morton Subotnick, and David Tudor, *Transmission Two: The Great Excursion* for chorus, computer music ensemble, and recorded dialogue was premiered by live broadcast from Hertz Hall on KPFA-FM in 1990. (Both Chowning and Charles Amirkhanian of KPFA, who had been instrumental in establishing the commissioning grant, were unfortunately not able to attend.)

"The recorded dialogue heard through the work chronicles episodes from conversations recorded between Austin and fellow composers reflecting on their own work as composers and music experimenters through the last thirty years of dramatic technological developments in the way music is created and presented.

Austin describes his work as "my 'sound movie':

"Central to the narrative continuity are choral settings and computer music transformations of select recorded aphorisms uttered spontaneously during the conversations, essences of the protagonists' aesthetics and compositional approaches. The role of the chorus in my 'sound movie' is as choric commentator, not unlike its role in classical Greek theater: musing poetically, reflecting philosophically, interjecting assertively, commenting amusedly, mocking 'rap-ingly', and interpreting between the protagonists of the ongoing dialogue and the audience."[27]

Specific soloists

Some identities are implicit in the purpose of the work, such as the saxophone pieces written for Stephen Duke, especially *BluesAx* (1995). Austin developed material to capture the musical personalities of renowned jazz saxophonists and of Duke himself. In addition to allowing him to improvise in performance, the piece uses Duke's own playing, as captured in a January, 1995, recording session in Denton, as a source for the processed and synthesized computer music.

"*BluesAx* is presented in seven continuous movements, four being interpretive portraits of the great jazz saxophonists Sidney Bechet, John Coltrane, Johnny Hodges, and Charlie Parker, these introduced and framed by three blues "choruses": I. BluesInCameroon; II. Sidney; III. Trane; IV. BluesLude; V. Hodges; VI. Cadenza; and VII.BluesOutParker.

"The montage of sounds and music heard on the tape includes saxophone sounds, my sine-tone "BluesHum" orchestra, rainforest and lakeside sounds recorded for the BBC in Kenya, Senegal, and Cameroon, as well as the city sounds of London's Soho, New York's Times Square, and New Orleans's Heritage Festival."[28]

The work is scored for soprano and alto saxophones, combined with the recorded computer music. The score is surprisingly precise, given the partly improvisatory nature of some of the sax material. It shows melodic ideas ("licks" to use the proper jazz term) to use as the starting point of the improvisation.

Figure 7: *BluesAx* score, excerpt

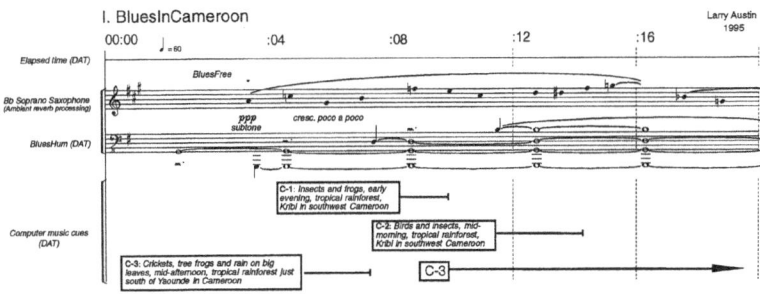

Figure 8: *BluesAx* score, excerpt

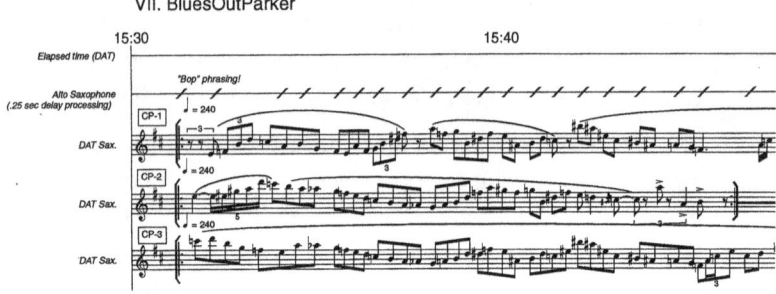

The work has become a contemporary classic of the saxophone repertoire, acclaimed for its savvy, sophis-ticated embodiment of saxophone stylings and for the lyric elegance of their blend with sonorous computer music sound. *BluesAx* brought Austin the distinction in 1996 of being the first American awarded the *Magistère* title at the International Electroacoustic Music Competition, Bourges, France.

A later work for saxophonist Duke, Austin's *Tableaux: Convolutions on a Theme* (2003), together with *BluesAx*, established Austin as a leading composer of cutting-edge saxophone music, adding to that instrument's expanding repertoire.

THE EXPERIMENTAL COMPOSER

Experiments in medium and materials

Austin would surely protest being categorized as a computer music composer. Unquestionably a leading pioneer in developing digital technology for serious composition, he would be the first to point to the computer as a tool, not a genre-defining medium. But it is a musical genre, with its own style trends, shared expertise (visible, for example, at International Computer Music Conferences and Society for Electro-Acoustic Music in the U.S. events), and a modest though avid audience. He would not argue with but embrace the designation as an experimental composer. This has to do more with idea, approach, and even purpose of the creative act.

A review of the approaches Austin has employed in a fresh or novel way demonstrates the diversity of his techniques:

- Fractals, algorithmic modeling
- Use of novel models such as coastline tracing
- Deep variations on or re-working of masterworks
- Blending/blurring real and virtual sound sources
- Environmental soundscapes
- Speech as both rhetorical and sonic material (a la John Cage)
- Sound diffusion, compositional control of spatial emanation
- Musical hybrids, mixing and fusing genres

These wide-ranging explorations of what a piece of music can be about of necessity led to innovative means of expression, both on a macro level of aesthetics and a micro level of notation.

Octophonics, convolutions, homages

A 2003 work, *Tableaux: Convolutions on a Theme (2003), for alto saxophone and octophonic computer music*, represents a culmination of several of these processes in Austin's work: convolutions; octophonics; and use of musical "themes" from older music.

Likewise, his program notes for the work provide a clear explanation of those processes as they shape a resulting aesthetic product that may epitomize Austin's unique 21st-century style.

> 'The soloist's sounds are amplified, processed, and diffused in the listening space, combined with the synchronized playback of ... computer music heard in a three-dimensional, octophonic montage: the listener is surrounded and immersed in the *live* and *recorded* sounds.

> "All of the sonic materials for *Tableaux* originated from Duke's saxophone recordings ... Through a process of pairing Duke's recordings, using one sound recording as the "primary input" file and a second recording as the "impulse response" file, the "convolution" process multiplies the waveform spectra of the two files together, producing a third, hybrid soundfile. The effect is a type of cross-synthesis, in which the common frequencies are reinforced. To the composer's ears, provocatively beautiful, ethereal sounds result: *tableaux sonore*...sonic images...passing before our ears.

> "The 'convolutions on a theme' are all based on a familiar theme and its harmonization composed originally as part of a 19th century composer's piano work, later brilliantly

orchestrated by a twentieth century composer. Now, a 21st century composer elaborates."[29]

Figure 9: *Tableaux: Convolutions on a Theme*, page 3

The overall effect, like so many other early Austin pieces (*Canadian Coastlines, ...art is self-alteration is Cage is...*) and later pieces (*Adagio, Threnos*) is (dare it be said about experimental music?) beautiful. As Austin wrote in his sketchbooks: "In sonority there is delicacy, richness, simplicity."[30]

Experiments in notation

If the exotic looking score of *...art is self-alteration is Cage is...* represents the apex of Austin's notational experiments, the roots appear far earlier. Certainly *Source* magazine was full of all kinds of experiments in how to express the concept or the detail of a musical idea.

More practical experiments with Austin's own pieces may have started as early as *Continuum: Open Style for a Number of*

Instruments (1964), in which time was represented by spatial proportion rather than by meter and note values. Accidentals were eliminated by making the round note-heads either open . . . white (for the "white-key" notes of the C scale), filled in black (for sharps), or half-filled for quarter-tone inflections of regular pitches. In *Catharsis*, a 1965 improvisational piece, instructions to performers are all verbal.

Each performer's part for *Canadian Coastlines* looks conventional enough, except for the tempo marking, "quarter note = 1 click". There is no conductor and thus no collected score, only synchronized click-track tapes.

In *Variations...Beyond Pierrot* elapsed time is similarly represented spatially with time measurements from the recorded computer music. Recitations heard in this pre-recorded material are notated as text. Each performer's "moon score" shows relative density of improvisational activity by fanciful moon-ovals that are either boldface, lighter in line, or mixed – a simple graphic analog. (See figure 2, page xx.)

Austin's 21st-century scores (as with so much in the art of this new millennium) tend to be simpler, reduced to essentials. The sustained sounds of *Threnos* are just whole notes tied to each other or tied to nothing, suggesting (like a cymbal or gong allowed to ring on) expansive sounds of indeterminate length. (See Figure 1, page xx.)

Perhaps with the exception of *...art is self-alteration is Cage is...*, notation for Austin is a means to an end, a necessary way of conveying instructions to performers. The particular mode of representation is chosen to fit the parameter(s) of most critical importance in a level of detail that is no less but also no more than needed for the musical concept. This functional approach does not imply casualness, as the execution of the notation, especially in the later works (most professionally engraved by former student Timothy Crowley) is precise and, at times, beautiful.

FIGURE 10: ...*art is self alteration is Cage is...* full score

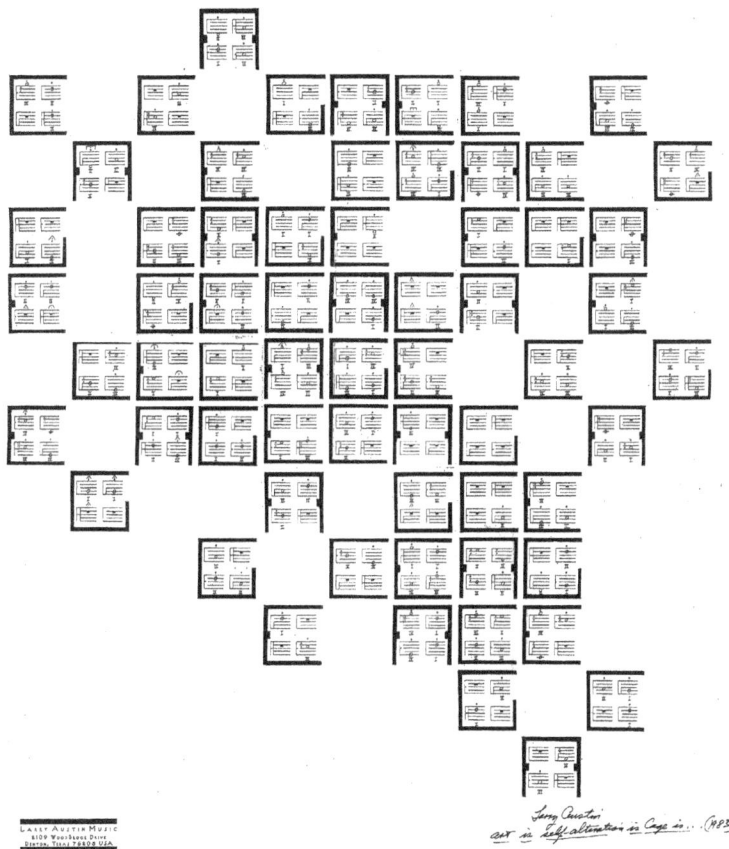

Experiments in improvisation and form

It may be just historical coincidence that Austin's first big success was a piece called *Improvisations* – but probably not. From jazz to the small ensemble experiments in Davis, Rome, and elsewhere, to later solo and chamber works, improvisation has been a major impetus of Austin's musical imagination. As with other major 20th-century experimental composers such as

Stockhausen, precision and spontaneity are polar sources of energy flow.

To discuss Form in the context of an experimental composer may require defining the term. Turning to the words of Austin himself and his co-author in their book *Learning to Compose*:

> "In music, form is the shaping of musical time through change. Form is the wholeness in time of a piece. Form is all the attributes the composer gives a piece, its whole sonic and temporal effect, its essence."[31]

In Chapter 2, "Form Modeling," Austin and Clark describe this grand sum of a composer's work in terms such as modeling processes, relating forces, architecture, trajectory, and continuity. Though this sounds complex, and can be, many of Austin's own form products are simple, some even elemental. *Sonata Concertante* has a Capo, Cadenza, and Coda. Most are even simpler, monolithic and continuous from beginning to end. The *Quadrants* series involves a huge arch, starting low and continuously rising in pitch to a summit, then continuously falling back down. *Canadian Coastlines* is one dense but gentle contrapuntal texture, eight continuous strolls on coastlines, from beginning to end.

Austin mused on such form in his sketches for *Sonata Concertante*: "Multi-dimensional form . . . interplay on complex time-scales."[32] In fact, there are very few pauses in Austin's music. It is perhaps the essence of experimentalism in art that each piece is one experiment, one set of initial conditions worked out to produce a methodical exploration of their possible ramifications – a notion of musical form both densely complex and at the same time monolithically simple.

This may be why some, such as the well-known composer who told Austin that his music was "not my cup of tea," find his music impenetrable. Others less fixed on finding a narrative story in music and more willing to amble aimlessly but observantly on a beach find Austin's music fascinating, compelling, and at times quite beautiful.

Impact and influence

Unquestionably Larry Austin has had a strong influence on the art of music through two strong currents in his career: his longtime career as a professor and mentor to many bright and now successful younger composers; and his leadership in organizations to advance the cause of making and disseminating new serious music. But what of the impact of his own writing, his own creations?

Virtually all the major trends of 20th-century music show up in Larry Austin's body of work. That seems to make him either a pioneer or an eclectic. Clearly he is an educated composer, well versed in the works of great masters. He admired, met and interacted with many: Bernstein, Foss, Stockhausen, Subotnick, Ashley, etc. He learned much from some: Milhaud, Cage, Ives. But his music is never derivative, always remarkably, perhaps obsessively original. If he ended up doing what others were also doing, it is because he was swimming in the same waters . . . and at the cutting edge of the wave.

Einstein was a theorist and a visionary, but not an experimentalist. It took generations of physicists crafting experiments with painstaking precision to prove with empirical certainty the accuracy or workability of his theories. Schoenberg was both a theorist and a consummate craftsman. Ives was at heart an inventor and a visionary explorer, widening for himself and others the range of musical possibilities by asking "what if?" and then trying it out. Cage was an experimenter, keen to construct a musical experiment and then content to observe and accept the results. Austin is some of all these: theorist, inventor, craftsman, experimenter, visionary explorer.

At the risk of seeming to invoke Freud gratuitously, each of the others had a fixation, perhaps an obsession. For Einstein it was relativity in space/time; for Schoenberg it was logic and coherence. For Ives it was the near chaos of multiplicity – of tempos and tonalities; for Cage, receptiveness – to chance, to singular sounds and ideas in a free environment of time and space. What are Austin's obsessions?

His titles hint at some recurring themes: improvisation; real vs. virtual/synthetic; open form; sound in space. A former jazz player then band director, he dove ardently into the development of electronics and then computers and now composes nothing without the latest technology at his fingertips. Yet he still crafts with those tools in the eternal realms of music: sound, time, and imagination. In Ives' words:

> "... the only known is the unknown, the only hope of humanity is the unseen spirit – what can't be done but what reaching out to do (as we feel like trying it) is to cast ... a 'universe of tones'."[33]

An explorer on the boundary of the familiar and the exotic, an experimenter on the cutting edge of possibility – Larry Austin is indeed the composer's composer.

"One may fly if one is willing to give up walking."

– John Cage[34]

ENDNOTES

1. L. Austin, T. Clark. *Learning to Compose: Modes Materials, and Models of Musical Invention.* Wm C. Brown Publishers, Dubuque, Iowa, 1989.

2. L. Austin, S. Lunetta, A. Woodbury, editors. *Source: Music of the Avant-Garde* Composer/Performer Edition, Davis and Sacramento, California, 1967-73.

3. L. Austin, D. Kahn, N. Gurusinghe, editors. *Source: Music of the Avant-Garde* University of California Press, Berkeley, California, 2011.

4. Larry Austin Selected Program Notes, htt://cemi.music.unt.edu/larry_austin/LApnotes.htm

5. ibid

6. *Percussive Notes*, Vol. 23, No. 6, Sept. 1985, pp. 58-84.

7. Larry Austin Selected Program Notes

8. L. Austin, "John Cage's *Williams Mix*," *A Handbook to Twentiet Century Musical Sketches*, edited by P. Hall, F. Sallis, Cambridc University Press, 2004, pp. 189-214.

9. from Larry Austin's personal copy

10. John Cage. *Silence.* MIT Press, Cambridge, Mass., 1961/66, p. 85.

11. J. *Cage*, R. *Kostalanetz. Conversing with Cage.* New York: Limelight Editions, 1981.

12. L. Austin, "John Cage's *Williams Mix*," *A Handbook to Twentieth-Century Musical Sketches*, edited by P. Hall, F. Sallis, Cambridge University Press, 2004, pp. 189-214.

13. Larry Austin Selected Program Notes

14. J. Strawn, *Computer Music Journal*, Vol. 6, No. 2, 1982, p. 14.

15. Clark, "Duality of Process and Drama in Larry Austin's Sonata Concertante," *Perspectives of New Music*, Vol. 23, No.1, 1984, pp. 114-115.
16. Larry Austin Selected Program Notes
17. ibid
18. ibid
19. ibid
20. ibid
21. ibid
22. ibid
23. ibid
24. ibid
25. ibid
26. ibid
27. ibid
28. ibid
29. ibid
30. Clark, "Duality of Process and Drama" p. 113.
31. *Learning to Compose*, p. 231.
32. Clark, "Duality of Process and Drama" p. 117.
33. Ives, from Austin's notes
34. "Experimental Music" from *Silence*, MIT Press, Cambridge, Mass., 1961/66, p. 9.

LARRY AUSTIN TIMELINE

1930	born in Duncan, Oklahoma, September 12
1937	moved to Vernon, Texas, with family
1939	started playing the trumpet
1941	joined Vernon High School Band at age 11
1947	Graduated from Vernon High School
1947	enrolled at North Texas State Teachers College, Denton
1948	began composing
1950	began formal composition study with Violet Archer
1951	completed Bachelor of Music at NTSTC
1952	completed Master of Music at NTSTC
	joined Fourth Army Band, San Antonio
1953	married Edna Navarro in San Antonio
1954	birth of son Don
1955	moved to California for Ph.D. musicology study at UC-Berkeley, became concert band teaching assistant, studied composition with Andrew Imbrie
	studied for six weeks with Darius Milhaud at Mills College
	birth of daughter Elizabeth
1957	birth of son David
1958	took a faculty position at UC-Davis
	son John Matthew born and died on same day
1959	*Homecoming: A Cantata for Soprano and Jazz Quintet*
1960	birth of daughter Thais
	Fantasy on a Theme by Berg
	Piano Variations

1961	first residency at MacDowell Colony
1962	birth of daughter Aurora
	met Leonard Bernstein at MacDowell Colony
	A Broken Consort
1964	Bernstein performed *Improvisations* with New York Philharmonic
	awarded tenure at UC-Davis
	Continuum: Open Style for a Number of Instruments
	Current
	Piano Set in Open Style
	Quartet in Open Style
1964-65	UC Creative Arts grant residency in Rome
1965	birth of daughter Helen Louise (died 1969)
	Changes: Open Style for Trombone and Tape
	Catharsis: Open Style for One Large and One Small Improvisation Ensemble, Tape, and Conductor
	Open Style for Orchestra with Piano Soloist
	Roma: A Theater Piece in Open Style for Improvisation Ensemble and Tape
	RomaDue: Sounds and Movements for Improvisation Ensemble, Dancers, and Tape
1966-67	met and hosted Stockhausen and David Tudor in Davis
	Bass: A Theater Piece in Open Style for String Bass, Player, Tape, and Film
	The Maze: A Theater Piece in Open Style for Three Percussionists, Dancer, Tapes, Machines, and Projections
1967	founded *Source: Music of the Avant-Garde*
	Accidents
1968	designated Distinguished Alumnus of North Texas State (University of North Texas)

1969	hosted John Cage in Davis
	Caritas
1970	promoted to full professor at UC-Davis
1971	*Agape Set*
	Prelude and Postlude to Plastic Surgery
	Quartet Three
	Quartet Four
1972	accepted position as music department chair at University of South Florida, Tampa
	Primal Hybrid
	Quadrants
	Quadrants: Event/Complex No. 1, 2, 3, 4
1973	co-founded Systems Complex for Studio and Performing Arts, USF
	Nineteen seventy-six
	Quadrants: Event/Complex No. 6, 7, 8
	Tableaux Vivants
1974	*Phoenix*
	Quadrants: Event/Complex No. 9
1975	*First Fantasy on Ives's Universe Symphony–The Earth*
1976	*Charley's Cornet*
	Quadrants: Event/Complex No. 10
	Second Fantasy on Ives's Universe Symphony–The Heavens
1977	*Quadrants: Event/Complex No. 11*
1978	accepted professorship at North Texas State University, Denton (formerly NTSTC) to establish a computer music program
	Catalogo Sonoro–'Narcisso'
1979	*Catalogo Voce*
1980	*Ceremony*

	Protoforms: Fractals for Computer Band
1981	co-founded Center for Experimental Music and Intermedia, University of North Texas (former NTSU)
1981	MacDowell Colony residency
	director of International Computer Music Conference, Denton, Texas
	Protoforms: Fractals for 'Cello Choir and Computer Band
	Canadian Coastlines: Canonic Fractals for Musicians and Computer Band
1982	MacDowell Colony residency
	art is self-alteration is Cage is...
	Euphonia: A Tale of the Future
	*Stars
1983	*Beachcombers*
1984	*Life Pulse Prelude*
	Ludus Fractalis
	Sonata Concertante
	Tango Violento
1985	*Clarini!*
	Montage: Themes and Variations for Violin and Computer Music on Tape
1986	founded Consortium to Distribute Computer Music
	MacDowell Colony residency
	Sinfonia Concertante: A Mozartean Episode
1988	*Euphonia 2344: An Intermezzo in Five Scenes*
	Violet's Invention
1989	co-authored *Learning to Compose*
	AccidentsTwo: Sound Projections for Piano with Computer Music
	La Barbara: The Name/The Sounds/The Music

1990	*Transmission Two: The Great Excursion*
1991	*SoundPoemSet: Pauline Oliveros/Jerry Hunt/Morton Subotnick/David Tudor*
1993	completed his realization of Ives' *Universe Symphony*
	¡Rompido!
1993-96	served as chair of UNT Division of Composition Studies
1994	composer residencies in Banff, then Tokyo
1995	*BluesAx*
	Variations...beyond Pierrot, a sound-play
1996	awarded *Magistère* prize by International Institute for Electroacoustic Music, Bourges, France
	retired from University of North Texas
	composer residency at University of Birmingham, UK
	Shin-Edo: CityscapeSet
1997	*Djuro's Tree*
1998	composer residency at Rockefeller Center in Bellagio, Italy
	Singing!...the music of my own time
	¡Tárogató!
2000	residency in Electroacoustic Music Studios at the University of York, UK
	residency at International Institute for Electroacoustic Music, Bourges, France
	Ottuplo!
	Williams [re]Mix[ed]
2002	*Threnos*
2003	*Tableaux: Convolutions on a Theme*
2005	Master Artist in Residence at Atlantic Center for the Arts, New Smyrna Beach, Florida
	Adagio: Convolutions on a Theme by Mozart
2006	*Les Flûtes de Pan: Hommage à Debussy*

2007	*John Explains*
	Redux
2008	*ReduxTwo*
2009	Lifetime Achievement Award from Society for Electro-Acoustic Music in the United States
2010	80th-birthday celebration concert at UNT Center for Experimental Music and Intermedia, Denton, Texas
2011	Austin's 80th birthday year retrospective concert at the Issue Project Room, New York
	ReduxThree
2012	Austin realization/completion of Ives's "Universe Symphony" performed by the Nashville Symphony Orchestra in Carnegie Hall

COMPOSITIONS

Large instrumental ensembles

Universe Symphony (1974-93) 37' – *as realized and completed by Larry Austin, based on Charles Ives's sketches for his unfinished "Universe Symphony" (1911-51)*; expanded symphony orch: 4343/4441/perc (21)/hrp/pno (2)/cel/org(opt)/str; publ. Peermusic Classical; recordings: Centaur CRC 2205 (1994); col legno LC07989 (2003)

Sinfonia Concertante: A Mozartean Episode (1986) 17'

chamber orchestra, tape narrative: fl, ob, cl, bsn, hn, tpt, timp, hrp, pno, 2 vn, va, vc, db, tape; publ. Larry Austin Music; recordings: CDCM v.1—Centaur CRC2029 (1988)

Clarini! (1985) 4'

20-member tpt choir; publ. Larry Austin Music

Life Pulse Prelude (1974-84) 24'

– based on sketches for percussion orchestra music from Ives's unfinished "Universe Symphony"

20-member percussion orchestra; optionally, live plus recorded percussionists (1996); publ. Peermusic Classical; recordings: CDCM v.12-Centaur CRC 2133 (1992)

Protoforms: Fractals for 'Cello Choir and Computer Band (1981) 12'; 13 vc, tape

Quadrants: Event/Complex No. 1 (1972) 9'

symphonic wind ensemble: 2 picc, 6 fl (4 w/picc), 16 cl, alt cl, 2 bass cl, contra-alt cl, 2 bsn, contrabsn, 8 tpt, 4 hns, 6 tbn, 4 tuba, 4 db, 4 perc, tape; publ. Peermusic Classical

Agape Set (1971) 30'

jazz orchestra: 5 saxs, 5 tpts, 4 trbns, perc set, pno, db; publ. Larry Austin Music

Open Style for Orchestra with Piano Soloist (1965) 6'

pno soloist/3242/4331/perc (4)/str; publ. Larry Austin Music

Catharsis: Open Style for One Large and One Small Improvisation Ensemble, Tape, and Conductor (1965) 9'

large ens = sym orch or sym wind ens / small ens = 3 - 7 wnd, brass, perc, str, and/or kybd, tape; publ. Larry Austin Music

In Memoriam JFK (1964) 10'

symphonic wind ensemble: picc, 2 fls, Eb cl, 6 cls, bass cl, 2 alt saxs, tnr sax, bari sax, 2 obs, Eng hn, 2 bns, 6 tpts, 4 hns, euph, 3 tbns, tuba, 7 perc; publ. Larry Austin Music

Improvisations for Orchestra and Jazz Soloists (1961) 14'

3 soloists (tpt or alt sax; perc set, db)/2222/4331/tmp/perc (2)/pno (cel)/str (optional version without vlns); publ. MJQ Music; video cassette: "Leonard Bernstein's Young People's Concerts with the New York Philharmonic: Jazz in the Concert Hall," The Leonard Bernstein Society, c/o W.T.S., Inc.

Fantasy on a Theme by Berg (1960) 10'

jazz orchestra: 5 saxs, 5 tpts, 4 trbns, perc set, pno, db; publ. Larry Austin Music

Chamber Ensembles

Ottuplo! (1998-2000) 12'

four inter-episodes for real and virtual string quartets: Segnali e risposti; Ottacordi e ottavi; Presto e libero; Otta-dia, scampanio; commissioned by the Smith Quartet; publ. Larry Austin Music

RomaDue: Sounds and Movements for Improvisation Ensemble, Dancers, and Tape (1965, rev. 1997) 10'   commissioned by the New York New Music and Dance Ensemble, Esther Lamneck, director; publ. Larry Austin Music

Variations...beyond Pierrot, a sound-play (1993-95) 30'

sopr, fl/picc, cl/bass cl, vn, vc, pno, electronics/tape; publ. Larry Austin Music

Beachcombers (1983) 20'-30'

live-electronic music for four musicians, tape, DL; recording: CDCM v.9 Centaur CRC 2078 (1991); publ. Larry Austin Music

...art is self-alteration is Cage is... (1982) 10'-15'

db quartet (optional db ensemble in multiples of 4 or db soloist with tape); recording: "A Chance Operation: The John Cage Tribute," Koch International Classics, 3-7238-2 Y6x2 (1993); publ. Larry Austin Music

Canadian Coastlines: Canonic Fractals for Musicians and Computer Band (1981) 10'

eight musicians: tape plus optional combinations of voices, strs, wnds, perc, kybds; publ. Larry Austin Music; recording: CDCM v.19 Centaur CRC 2219

Second Fantasy on Ives's Universe Symphony-The Heavens (1976) 17'

cl, va, pno/cel, perc, tape; publ. Larry Austin Music

First Fantasy on Ives's Universe Symphony-The Earth (1975) 17'; brass (4 tpts, 2 hns, 4 trbns, 2 tubas), narrator, tape; publ. Larry Austin Music

Tableaux Vivants (1973, rev. 1981) 13'

4-6 musicians (optional combinations of strs, wnds, perc, kybds, voices), tape, slides; publ. Larry Austin Music

The Maze: A Theater Piece in Open Style for Three Percussionists, Dancer, Tapes, Machines, and Projections (1966) 31'; publ. Larry Austin Music

Roma: A Theater Piece in Open Style for Improvisation Ensemble and Tape (1965) 16'

optional combinations of 3 - 5 wind, brass, perc, strings, keyboard; publ. Larry Austin Music

Quartet in Open Style (1964) 20'

2 vln, va, vc; publ. Larry Austin Music

Continuum: Open Style for a Number of Instruments (1964) 12'

optional combinations of fl/alt fl, ob/Eng hn, bn/cbn, tpt/Flglhn, db, perc, hpschd/cel publ. publ. Larry Austin Music

A Broken Consort (1962) 13'

fl, cl, tpt, hn, pno, cb, dr set; publ. MJQ Music

Homecoming: A Cantata for Soprano and Jazz Quintet (1958-9) 10'

tpt, tnr sax, pno, db, drum set; publ. Larry Austin Music

Soloist with tape/electronics

ReduxThree (2010-11)

clarinet solo, duo, quartet, or octet, video and octophonic computer music; publ. Larry Austin Music

ReduxTwo (2008) 7'30"

piano and octophonic computer music; commissioned by pianist Joseph Kubera, premiere Feb. 12, 2009, Roulette Intermedium, New York City, publ. Larry Austin Music

Redux (2007) 7'30"

violin and octophonic computer music; commissioned by violinist Patricia Strange, premiere performance May 14, 2007, Recital Hall, University of Maryland, Baltimore County; publ. Larry Austin Music

Les Flûtes de Pan: Hommage à Debussy (2006) 7'30"

flute (piccolo), octophonic computer music, and dancers (optional); commissioned by flutist Jacqueline Martelle, premiere March 15, 2007, Experimental Intermedia Foundation, New York; publ. Larry Austin Music

Adagio: Convolutions on a Theme by Mozart (2005) 10'

clarinet and computer; commissioned by clarinetist F. Gerard Errante, premiere Oct. 27, 2005, 26th Annual New Music & Art Festival, MidAmerican Center for Contemporary Music, Bowling Green State University, Bowling Green, Ohio.; publ. Larry Austin Music

Tableaux: Convolutions on a Theme (2003) 16'

alto saxophone and octophonic computer music; commissioned by saxophonist Stephen Duke, premiere Feb. 10, 2004, Recital Hall, Northern Illinois University, DeKalb; publ. Larry Austin Music

Threnos (2001-2002) 7'30"

1, 2, 4, or 8 bass clarinets, real (live) and virtual (computer/ADAT), with octophonic computer music; commissioned by bass clarinetist Michael Lowenstern; premiered Jan. 30, 2003, Interpretations Series concert at Merkin Concert Hall, New York, NY; publ. Larry Austin Music

¡Tárogató! (1998) 11'

tárogató (opt. cl, sop sax, or bass cl), dancer(s), and octophonic computer music (opt. stereo tape); commissioned by New York New Music and Dance Ensemble, Esther Lamneck, director

Singing!...the music of my own time (1996-98) 25'

a sound-portrait of singer Thomas Buckner with octophonic computer music on ADAT, interpreted as a sound-play, in three parts, by Thomas Buckner, baritone voice; commissioned by Thomas Buckner; publ. Larry Austin Music

BluesAx (1995) 19'

saxophonist (sop/alt saxs), tape/electronics [Magisterium Prize, Bourges, 1996]

recording: Cultures Electroniques 9, GMEB, Mnemosyne Musicque Media, CD278060/61 (1997)

Quadrants: Event/Complex No. 4 (1972, rev. 1994) 9'

Pianist, Yamaha Disclavier piano, tape/electronics; publ. Larry Austin Music

recording: CDCM v.19 Centaur CRC 2219 (1994)

AccidentsTwo: Sound Projections for Piano with Computer Music (1992) 20'

pianist and tape/electronics; recording: V. 19, CDCM v.19, Centaur CRC 2219 (1994); publ. Larry Austin Music

La Barbara: The Name/The Sounds/The Music (1991) 23'; voice with computer music; recording: CDCM v.13, Centaur CRC 2166 (1993); publ. Larry Austin Music

Montage: Themes and Variations for Violin and Computer Music on Tape (1985) 13'; publ. Semar Editore, Rome; recording: CDCM v.10, Centaur CRC 2110 (1991)

Sonata Concertante (1983-4) 11'

pno, tape; publ. Borik Press; recording: CDCM v.1, Centaur CRC 2029 (1988)

Catalogo Sonoro-'Narcisso' (1978) 10'

viola, tape; publ. Larry Austin Music

Quadrants: Event/Complex Nos. 11 (1977), *10* (1976), *9* (1974), *8, 7, 6, 4, 3* (1973) 9' each; respectively: db, trbn, perc, vla, fl, cl, vc, pno, vln; performed singly or in any combination with Quadrants tape; publ. Larry Austin Music

Prelude and Postlude to Plastic Surgery (1971) 15'

film and theatre piece: pno/electronic kybd, film, tape; publ. Larry Austin Music

Accidents (1967) 20'

a theater piece for electronically prepared pno; recording: CDCM v.19, Centaur CRC 2219 (1994); publ. Larry Austin Music; recording: lp: DL, Source Records, SR13 (1968)

Bass: A Theater Piece in Open Style for String Bass, Player, Tape, and Film (1966) 11'

Changes: Open Style for Trombone and Tape (1965) 10'; publ. Larry Austin Music

Tape/computer music

Williams [re]Mix[ed] (1997-2000) 19 - 23 min

for octophonic computer music system (ADAT), based on John Cage's *Williams Mix* (1951-53), for eight magnetic tapes; The Theme Restored; Six Short Variations: A-city sounds, B-country sounds, C-electronic sounds, D-manually produced sounds, E-wind produced sounds, F-small sounds; The Nth Realization; commissioned by International Institute for Electroacoustic Music, Bourges, France, with sponsorship and support from the John Cage Trust and C. F. Peters Corporation; publ. Larry Austin Music

John Explains (2007) 9'46"

octophonic computer music; publ. Larry Austin Music

Djuro's Tree (1997) 12'30"

octophonic computer music, ADAT, commissioned and published by Borik Press

Shin-Edo: CityscapeSet (1994-96) 20'

Ikebukuro/Sunshine City – Rikugien Garden – Kunitachi morning- "Tamagawa-josui desu." - Shinjuku/Ginza; publ. Borik Press

¡Rompido! (1993) 25'

GraniteHarp - ThunderStone – SteleMusic

publ. Borik Press; recording: CDCM v.24, Centaur CRC 2310 (1997)

SoundPoemSet: Pauline Oliveros/Jerry Hunt/Morton Subotnick/David Tudor (1990-91) 19'; publ. Borik Press; recording: CDCM v.16, Centaur CRC2193 (1994)

Ludus Fractalis (1984) 11'
video tape composition; publ. Borik Press

*Stars (1982); 8'; publ. Larry Austin Music

Protoforms: Fractals for Computer Band (1980) 10'
publ. Larry Austin Music

Phoenix (1974) 10'; publ. Larry Austin Music

Nineteen seventy-six (1973) 16'; publ. Larry Austin Music

Quadrants (1972) 9'; publ. Larry Austin Music

Primal Hybrid (1972) 11'; publ. Larry Austin Music

Quartet Four (1971) 8'; publ. Larry Austin Music

Quartet Three (1971) 12'; publ. Larry Austin Music

Caritas (1969) 30'
publ. Larry Austin Music; recording: LP, Source Records, SR17, Deep Listening (1970)

Instrumental solo/duo

Violet's Invention (1988) 4'
piano; publ. Larry Austin Music

Tango Violento (1984) 3'
piano; publ. Larry Austin Music

Charley's Cornet (1976) 5'
cornet, piano; publ. Peermusic Classical; recording: Crystal Records CD763 (2004)

Current (1964) 10'
cl, pno; publ. Larry Austin Music

Piano Set in Open Style (1964) 10'
publ. Larry Austin Music

Piano Variations (1960) 10'
publ. MJQ Music

Chorus/opera/voice

Transmission Two: The Great Excursion (1989-90) 107'
in seven episodes; chorus, vc, pno/kbd, perc, tape; ; publ. Larry Austin Music; recording: CDCM v.15, Centaur CRC 2190 (1994)

Euphonia 2344: An Intermezzo in Five Scenes (1988) 45'
Thomas Holliday, librettist; SATB quartet, tape; publ. Larry Austin Music

Euphonia: A Tale of the Future (1981-82) 2 hours

opera in two acts based on Hector Berlioz's tale of the "Twenty-fifth Evening" from his "Evenings with the Orchestra"; Thomas Holliday, librettist; principals: sop, mezzo-sop, contralto, ten, bass; SATB chorus; chamber orch: 1111/ 111/ timp/ perc/ pno/ hrp/str (54321), tape; publ. Larry Austin Music

Ceremony (1980) 15'

soprano or tenor, organ; publ. Larry Austin Music

Catalogo Voce (1979) 11'

a mini-opera for bass-baritone, tape, slides; publ. Larry Austin Music

Quadrants: Event/Complex No. 2 (1972) 9'

chorus, tape; publ. Larry Austin Music

RECORDINGS

Compact discs

Pogus Productions, P210502 (2008) 50 Ayr Rd, Chester, NY, 10918

Source Records 1-6, Music of the AvantGarde, 1968-1971: The Digital Reissue of the Source LPs on a 3-Compact Disc Set, including Larry Austin's *Accidents* and *Caritas*

Centaur Records, CRC2830 (2006)

"The Composer in the Computer Age X," Volume 35, CDCM Computer Music Series

Ottuplo!, Flux Quartet, ambisonic recording by Smith Quartet, in concert January 30, 2003, Merkin Concert Hall, New York City, Interpretations Series presented by World Music Institute and Thomas Buckner;

Adagio: Convolutions on a Theme by Mozart, F. Gerard Errante, clarinet;

RomaDue;

Tableaux: Convolutions on a Theme, Stephen Duke, alto saxophone;

art is self-alteration is Cage is..., performed/recorded by Robert Black, contrabass;

Threnos, in memory of the victims of September 11, 2001, Michael Lowenstern, bass clarinet;

Les Flûtes de Pan: Hommage à Debussy, Jacquiline Martelle, flute/piccolo

Crystal Records CD763 (2004)

"UNconventional Trumpet" *Charley's Cornet*, John Holt, cornet, Natalia Bolshakova, piano

col legno WWE 1CD 20074 (2003)

Charles Ives's Universe Symphony (1911-1951), as realized and completed by Larry Austin (1974-93) for multiple orchestras, in three continuous sections, based on Charles Ives's sketches for his unfinished *Universe Symphony* (1911-51); Rundfunk-Sinfonieorchester Saarbrucken, Michael Stern, principal conductor, assistant conductors Larry Austin, Johannes Kalitzke, Michael Schmidtsdorff, and Christian Voss, recorded broadcast, Music in the Twentieth Century Festival, Saarbrucken, Germany, May 24, 1998

Society for Electro-Acoustic Music in the U.S., Music from SEAMUS XIII (2003)

Threnos, for real and virtual bass clarinets, commissioned and recorded by bass clarinetist Michael Lowenstern

Romeo Records (2002)

"Esther Lamneck, Tárogató!, A Folk Instrument With a Contemporary Sound" *Tárogató!*, recorded/processed tárogató

Electronic Music Foundation Ltd., EMF 039 (2001) 116 No. Lake Ave., Albany, NY 12206

Octo-Mixes, Larry Austin, "Octophonic Computer Music, 1996-2001" *Tárogató!* commissioned by Esther Lamneck, recorded/processed tárogató;

Stephen Duke, soprano saxophone soloist. Tárogató recording, New York University studio, Paul Geluso, engineer, April 29,

1997. Saxophone recorded at DRM Productions, Dallas, Texas, Sept.7, 2001;

Singing!...the music of my own time, commissioned and recorded by Thomas Buckner, baritone. Interview and vocal material recorded in Buckner's private studio, New York City, Nov. 6, 1996, L. Austin, recording engineer;

Djuro's Tree (1997), commissioned by Borik Press in memory of Djuro Kurepa, mathematician. Interview of Alexandra Kurepa and Andre Waschka recorded in North Carolina, April 7, 1997, L. Austin, recording engineer. Computer music created in the Electroacoustic Music Studios, University of Birmingham, UK, June-July, 1997;

Williams [re]Mix[ed], based on John Cage's *Williams Mix*, commissioned by the International Institute for Electroacoustic Music, Bourges, France, with sponsorship and support from the John Cage Trust and C.F. Peters Corporation. Octophonic computer music program, *Williams [re]Mix[er]*, designed by Austin with Michael Thompson, programmer; Producers: Austin and Joel Chadabe. Annotators: James Dashow and L. Austin.

Centaur Records, CRC 2428 (1999)

"The Composer in the Computer Age–VIII: Larry Austin–SoundPlays, Cityscapes, SoundPortraits: 1993-96," Volume 28, CDCM Computer Music Series

Variations...beyond Pierrot, a sound-play in three parts, performed by Thira: Therese Costes, soprano; Laurel Ridd, flutes; Lori Freedman, clarinets; Paule Prefontaine, violin; Arkadiusz Tesarczyk, cello; Mary Jo Carrabre, piano; Michael Matthews, electronics;

Shin-Edo: CityscapeSet. Ikebukuro/Sunshine City –Rikugien Garden–Kunitachi morning–"Tamagawa-josui desu." – Shinjuku/Ginza;

BluesAx, I. BluesInCameroon; II. Sidney; III. Trane; IV. BluesLude; V. Hodges; VI. Cadenza; VII. BluesOutParker, Stephen Duke, soprano and alto saxophones

Centaur Records, CRC 2407 (1998)

"Music from CEMI, University of North Texas," Volume 27, CDCM Computer Music Series

Quadrants: Event/Complex No. 1, North Texas Wind Symphony, Eugene Corporon, conductor

Centaur Records, CRC 2310 (1997)

"The Composer in the Computer Age—VII," Volume 24, CDCM Computer Music Series

¡Rompido! Sound materials recorded on location at the Fred Jones Museum, Norman, Oklahoma; the Moroles studio, Rockport, Texas; and the Davis-Maclain Gallery, Houston, Texas; Larry Austin, producer and recording engineer

Cultures Electroniques/9, Serie GMEB/UNESCO/CIME, Bourges (1996)

BluesAx, Stephen Duke, saxophone;

Quadrants: Event/Complex No. 4 and *Event/Complex No. 9*, J. B. Floyd, pianist and Disclavier programmer, Robert McCormick, percussion

Centaur Records, CRC 2190 (1994)

Volume 15, CDCM Computer Music Series

Transmission Two: The Great Excursion "Max Mathews Episode," live recording, concert broadcast on KPFA-FM, Berkeley, CA, February 26, 1990, UC Chamber Chorus, Philip Brett, conductor;

Chris Brown, keyboards; Chris Chafe, celletto; William Winant, percussion and Radio Drum; Austin, Jay Kadis, Randall Packer, Todd Winkler, computer music systems; Austin, producer; Richard Friedman, KPFA-FM producer

Centaur Records, CRC 2219 (1994)

"The Composer in the Computer Age–IV, A Larry Austin Retrospective: 1967-94," Volume 19, CDCM Computer Music Series

AccidentsTwo: Sound Projections for Piano with Computer Music;

Canadian Coastlines: Canonic Fractals for Musicians and Computer Band;

Quadrants: Event/Complex No. 4, *Quadrants: Event/Complex No. 9*

Centaur Records, CRC 2205 (1994)

Charles Ives's Universe Symphony, as realized and completed by Larry Austin, premiere recording by the Cincinnati Philharmonia Orchestra, Gerhard Samuel, Music Director, with the Percussion Ensemble of the College-Conservatory of Music, made possible by the assistance of the American Academy and National Institute of Arts and Letters, the Charles Ives Society, Inc., and the Yale University Music Library.

Centaur Records, CRC 2193 (1994)

"The Composer in the Computer Age—II," Volume 16, CDCM Computer Music Series

SoundPoemSet, computer music on tape: 1 Pauline Oliveros; 2 Jerry Hunt; 3 Morton Subotnick; 4 David Tudor

Koch International Classics compact disc series, 3-7238-2 Y6x2 (1993) "A Chance Operation: The John Cage Tribute"

art is self-alteration is Cage is..., Robert Black, double bass; produced and mixed by Larry Austin, engineered by Bruce Elliott at Sound Situation in Glastonbury, CT

Centaur Records, CRC 2166 (1993)

"The Virtuoso in the Computer Age–III", Volume 13, CDCM Computer Music Series; *La Barbara: The Name/The Sounds/The Music*, Joan La Barbara, soprano

Leonardo Music Journal, Vol. 1, No. 1 (1992) compact disc; *Transmission Two: The Great Excursion*, "Morton Subotnick Episode"; University of California Chamber Chorus, Phillip Brett, conductor; Chris Chafe, celletto; Chris Brown, keyboards; William Winant, Boie Radio Drum and percussion

Centaur Records, Inc., CRC 2133 (1992)

"The Virtuoso in the Computer Age—II," Volume 12, CDCM Computer Music Series; *Life Pulse Prelude*, based on sketches and plans for percussion orchestra music from a portion of Charles Ives's unfinished Universe Symphony; The Percussion Group and guest soloists

Centaur Records, CRC 2110 (1991)

"The Virtuoso in the Computer Age–I," Volume 10, CDCM Computer Music Series; *Montage: Themes and Variations for Violin and Computer Music on Tape*, Robert Davidovici, violin

Centaur Records, CRC 2078 (1991)

Volume 9, CDCM Computer Music Series

Beachcombers, for four musicians and tape

Centaur Records, CRC 2029 (1988)

Volume 1, CDCM Computer Music Series

Sinfonia Concertante, chamber orchestra conducted by Thomas Clark;

Sonata Concertante, Adam Wodnicki, piano

Other media

Deep Listening Publications, LA-V-VHS video cassette (stereo) (1990)   *Ludus Fractalis*, a video composition

Folkways Records, FTS37475 (1983) "Computer Music"

Canadian Coastlines: Canonic Fractals for Musicians and Computer Band

IRIDA, 0022 (1980)   P.O. Box 240, Rt.1, Canton, TX 75103; "Larry Austin Hybrid Musics: Four Compositions"

Maroon Bells,

Catalogo Voce,

Quadrants: Event/Complex No. 1,

Second Fantasy on Ives' Universe Symphony

Advance Records, FGR9S (1974)

"New Music for Woodwinds"

Current, Phil Rehfeldt, clarinet, Thomas Warburton, piano

Advance Records, FGR10S (1970)

"Robert Floyd Plays New Piano Music by Hans Werner Henze and Larry Austin"

Piano Set in Open Style, Piano Variations

Source Records, SR17, Composer-Performer Edition (1970)

Caritas

Source Records, SR13, Composer-Performer Edition (1968)

Accidents for piano and live electronics, performed by David Tudor

Columbia Masterworks, MS6733 (1965)

"Leonard Bernstein Conducts Music of Our Time," New York Philharmonic

Improvisations for Orchestra and Jazz Soloists

NME Records, Composer-Performer Edition (1964)

"New Music Ensemble Free Group Improvisations"

BOOKS and BOOK CHAPTERS

L. Austin, "John Cage's *Williams Mix* (1951-53): The Restoration and New Realizations of and Variations on the First Octophonic, Surround-Sound Tape Composition"

in *A Handbook to Twentieth-Century Musical Sketches*, edited by Patricia Hall and Friedmann Sallis, ISBN 0 521 80860 X, Cambridge University Press, Cambridge, UK, 2004, pp. 189-214.

L. Austin, "The Realization and First Complete Performances of Ives's Universe Symphony"

in *Ives Studies*, edited by Philip Lambert, ISBN 0 521 582776, Cambridge University Press, Cambridge, UK, 1998, pp. 179-232.

Larry Austin, Thomas Clark. *Learning to Compose: Modes Materials, and Models of Musical Invention*. ISBN 0-697-03495-X, Wm C. Brown Publishers, Dubuque, Iowa, 1989.

L. Austin, D. Kahn, N. Gurusinghe, editors. *Source: Music of the Avant-Garde: 1966-1973*.

ISBN: 9780520257481, University of California Press, Berkeley, California, 2011.

Periodical

L. Austin, S. Lunetta, A. Woodbury, editors. *Source: Music of the Avant-Garde*
Issues 1-11. Composer/Performer Edition, Davis and Sacramento, California, 1967-73.

ARTICLES
by Larry Austin

"14th Florida Electroacoustic Music Festival, 2005"
Computer Music Journal, Vol. 29, No. 4, Winter, 2005, pp. 77-82.

"Center for Experimental Music and Intermedia: Forty Years on the Edge"
Computer Music Journal, Vol. 28, No. 4, Winter, 2004, pp. 85-87.

"John Cage/Lejaren Hiller: HPSCHD"
Computer Music Journal, Vol. 28, No. 3, Fall, 2004, pp. 83-85.

"Sound Diffusion in Composition and Performance II: An Interview with Ambrose Field"
Computer Music Journal, Vol. 25, No.4, winter, 2001, pp. 10-21.

"Synthese 1999"
Computer Music Journal, Vol. 24, No. 1, spring, 2000, pp. 70-74.

"Sound Diffusion in Composition and Performance: An Interview with Denis Smalley"

Computer Music Journal, Vol. 24, No. 2, summer, 2000, pp. 10-21.

"Living Tomorrow's Life: In Memoriam, Salvatore Martirano, 1927-1995"

Perspectives of New Music, Vol. 34, No. 1, winter, 1996, pp. 163-165.

"Modeling Music with Computers: Random Thoughts"

Proceedings of the 1993 International Computer Music Conference, Tokyo, Japan, Sept. 10-15, 1993, pp. 21-23.

"Modeling a Hypermedia Composition/Performance System"

Proceedings of the 1993 International Computer Music Conference, Tokyo, Japan, Sept. 10-15, 1993, pp. 198-201.

"Interview with John Cage and Lejaren Hiller: John Cage Remembered"

Computer Music Journal, V. 16, No. 4, Winter, 1992, pp. 15-29.

"Transmission Two: The Great Excursion: The Aesthetic, Art and Science of a Composition for Radio"

Leonardo Music Journal, Vol. 1, No. 1, 1992, pp. 81-88.

"John Cage Remembered"

ARRAY, Vol. 12, No. 4, 1992.

"1992 ICMC Report"
ARRAY, Vol. 12, No. 4, 1992, pp. 6-7.

"Goodbye to Kurt and Carla"
ARRAY, Vol. 12, No. 3, 1992, p. 1.

"Nominees Named for 1993 ICMA Commission Awards"
ARRAY, Vol. 12, No.2, 1992, pp. 2-3.

"1993 ICMA Commission Awards"
ARRAY, Vol. 12, No. 1, 1992, pp. 3-4.

"Live-Electronic Music on the Third Coast"
Contemporary Music Review, Vol. 6, Part 1, Fall, 1991, pp. 107-128.

"Report on the 1991 ICMC in Montreal, Oct. 16-20"
ARRAY, Vol. 11, No. 4, Fall, 1991, pp. 1-2.

"New Name, No More Debt, and the ICMA Commission Awards"
ARRAY, Vol. 11, No. 3, Summer, 1991.

"Women, Elitism, and the Computer Music Association"
ARRAY, Vol. 11, No. 2, Spring, 1991, pp. 11-12.

"State of the Association"
ARRAY, Vol. 11, No. 1, Winter, 1991, pp. 1-2.

"Highlights"

ARRAY, Vol. 10, No. 4, Fall, 1990, pp. 6-7.

"Live or Taped? Real or Unreal Time? Looking or Listening? Are These Issues Live or Dead?"

ARRAY, Vol. 10, No. 3, Summer, 1990, pp. 11-13.

"Inaugural Address to the Computer Music Association"

ARRAY, Vol. 10, No. 2, Spring, 1990, pp. 1-2.

"Live-Electronic Music on the Third Coast"

Contemporary Music Review, Vol. 6, Part 1, Fall, 1990.

"Electro-Acoustic Music in the United States"

Composer News: A Publication of the Texas Composers Forum, Vol. 2, No. 2, Spring, 1988, pp. 2,4.

"Electro-Acoustic Music in the USA"

Festival Booklet for the Elektronmusic Festival 1987, Skinnskatteberg/Uttersberg, pp. 6-7, 18, 1987.

"Report from Vancouver, the 1985 International Computer Music Conference"

Perspectives of New Music, Vol. 23, No. 2, 1985.

"Charles Ives's Life Pulse Prelude: A Realization for Modern Performance from Sketches for the Universe Symphony"

Percussive Notes: Research Edition, Vol. 23, No. 6, Sept., 1985, pp. 58-84.

"To Arms....Be Uncommon: Larry Austin interviews Larry Austin"

Ear Magazine, Vol. 8, No. 6, June, 1984.

"Phantasmagoria: Chronicle of Computer-assisted Composition/ Performance"

Proceedings of the 1982 International Computer Music Conference, Venice.

"SYCOM–Systems Complex for the Studio and Performing Arts",

Numus West, May, 1974, pp. 57-59.

"New Romanticism: an Emerging Aesthetic for Electronic Music, Pt. II"

Mundus Artium, Journal of International Literature and the Arts, Vol. VI, No. 2, 1973, pp. 96-102.

"New Romanticism: an Emerging Aesthetic for Electronic Music, Pt. 1"

Mundus Artium, Journal of International Literature and the Arts, Vol. VI, No. 1, 1973, pp. 183-189.

"Can Electronic Music Be Romantic?"

New York Times, Sept. 17, 1971.

"Editorial" reprints of articles from the *New York Times*
SOURCE, Vol.4, Issues 7-8, Jan.-July, 1970, pp. 55-58.

"Music is Dead, Long Live Music"
New York Times, July 6, 1969, D13-D14.

"Music Only for the Privileged?"
New York Times, Sept.1, 1968, D11, D12.

"Music and Light"
ARTSCANADA, Dec., 1968, p. 61.

"Groups"
SOURCE, Vol. 2, No. 1, 1968, pp. 14-27.

"Is the Concerto Dead? Yes"
New York Times, March 10, 1968, pp. M1, M3.

"Is the Composer Anonymous?"
SOURCE, Vol. 1, No. 2, 1967, pp. 1-3.

"Conversation: Karlheinz Stockhausen, Robert Ashley, Larry Austin", *SOURCE*, Vol. 1, No. 1, 1967, pp.104-8.

Co-authored

L. Austin, R. Waschka II, "Computer Music for Compact Disc: Composition, Production, Audience," *Computer Music Journal*, Vol. 20, No. 2, summer, 1996, pp. 17-27.

L. Austin, R. Waschka II, "Composing Computer Music for Compact Disc: A Practicum", *Proceedings of the 1992 International Computer Music Conference*, San Jose, California, Fall, 1992, pp. 469-472.

L. Austin, C. Boone, X. Serra, "Transmission Two: The Great Excursion (TT:TGE): The Aesthetic, Art and Science of a Composition for Radio", *Leonardo Music Journal*, Vol.1 No. 1, 1991, 81-88.

L. Austin, E. De Lisa, "Modeling Processes of Musical Invention", *Proceedings of the 1987 International Computer Music Conference*, Champaign, Illinois: University of Illinois, 1988.

L. Austin, B. Childs, "Forum: Improvisation", *Perspectives of New Music*, Vol. 21, Nos. 1-2, 1982-83, pp. 26-34.

L. Austin, L. Bryant, "A Computer-synchronized, Multi-track Recording System", *Proceedings,* Second Annual Music Computation Conference, 1975.

L. Austin, J. Cage, L. Hiller, "HPSCHD", *SOURCE*, Vol. 2, No. 2, 1968, pp. 10-19.

OTHER SOURCES

John Cage: *Silence*. Cambridge, Massachusetts: The MIT Press, 1966.

Thomas Clark, "Duality of Process and Drama in Larry Austin's *Sonata Concertante*"
Perspectives of New Music, xxiii/1 (1984), 112-25.

Thomas Clark, "Coasts: on the Creative Edge"
Computer Music Journal, xiii/1 (1989), 21-35.

Thomas Clark, "Larry Austin"
Contemporary Composers, Morton & Collins, ed. London: St. James Press, 1992.

Anthony Cornicello, "An Interview with Larry Austin, Part 1"
SEAMUS Newsletter, Issue 2, June, 2009.

David Ernst: *The Evolution of Electronic Music*. New York, Schirmer Books, 1977.

David Ewen: *American Composers: a Biographical Dictionary*. New York: G.P. Putnam's Sons, 1982.

A. Kennedy, "Sound-Script Relations and the New Notation"
Artform, xii/1 (1973), 38.

Elainie Lillios, "An Interview with Larry Austin"
Journal SEAMUS, Vol. 20, No. 1, Spring, 2009.

Elainie Lillios, "*OCTO MIXES* (review)"
Computer Music Journal, Vol. 28, No. 3, Fall 2004, 86-88.

Zachary Lyman, "Completing Ives's Universe Symphony: An Interview with Larry Austin"
American Music, Vol. 26, No. 4, Winter, 2008.

Benoit Mandelbrot: *The Fractal Geometry of Nature*. San Francisco: Freeman and Co., 1982.

Dary John Mizelle, "Larry Austin at Experimental Intermedia", *Journal SEAMUS*, Vol. 19, No. 2, 2007.

James Phelps, "Ottuplo! Larry Austin: The Eighth Decade. SoundPortraits * Convolutions * Cityscape"; Centaur Records - CRC 2830; reviewed by Jim Phelps, Northern Illinois University, USA", *Computer Music Journal*, Vol. 31, No. 2, Summer, 2007.

John Vinton: *Dictionary of Contemporary Music*. New York: E.P. Dutton & Co., 1971.

Walter Zimmermann: *Desert Plants: Conversations with 23 American Musicians*. Vancouver: A.R.C. Publications, 1976.

Web sites

Larry Austin's Home Page -

http://cemi.music.unt.edu/larry_austin/

Consortium to Distribute Computer Music -
http://music.unt.edu/CDCM

INDEX

Accidents, 47, 72, 84, 89, 96
Accidents Two, 27, 74, 83, 93
algorithmic, 37, 38, 45, 54, 61
ambisonic, 23, 54, 55, 89
American Academy and National Institute of Arts and Letters, 35,93
Amirkhanian, 57
analog synthesizers, 47
Ann Arbor, 18
Archer, Violet, 4, 5, 10, 71
architecture, 8, 66
Army Band, 6, 71
array, 45
Array, 99-101
...art is self alteration is Cage is...., 37, 43-46, 63-65, 74, 79, 89, 94
Ashley, Robert, 17, 19, 24, 57, 67, 103
Aspen, 20, 39
Atlantic Center for the Arts, 10, 24, 75
Austin,
  Aurora, 14, 72
  David, 14, 71
  Don, 7, 10, 14, 71
  Edna (Navarro), viii-ix, 6, 8, 10, 12, 21, 25, 71
  Elizabeth, 7, 14, 18, 71
  Helen Louise, 72
  Thais, 14, 71
avant-garde, 7, 12, 69, 72, 97, 98

Banff Center for the Arts, 23
Bartok, Bela, 4-5, 32-33
Beachcombers, 16, 42-44, 56, 74, 79, 97-98
Bechet, Sidney, 59
Beethoven, Ludwig van, 8, 30
Beijing, 24
Bellagio, 24, 54-55, 75
Berdahl, James, 7
Berg, Alban, 5, 71, 79

Berkeley, 4, 7-11, 13-14, 16, 28, 40, 57, 69, 71, 92, 97
Berlin, 23
Bernstein, Leonard, v, 11-12, 28, 67, 72, 78, 96
Bertucini, Mario, 13, 15
Blank, Ernest, 8
BluesAx, 58-60, 75, 83, 92
Blum, Thom, 48
BMI, 6, 11-12, 28
Boosey & Hawkes, 52
Borik Press, viii, 52, 84-86, 91
Boston, 48
Bourges, 23-24, 39, 60, 75, 83, 85, 91-92
Box, Euell, 3
Brown,
  Chris, 93-94
  Earle, 37-38
  Newel Kay, 21
  Wm C., 22, 69, 97
Brubeck, Dave, 9
Bryant,
  Allen, 13, 15
  L. 104
Buchla synthesizer, 47
Bukofzer, Manfred, 7

Cage, John, v, 4, 15-16, 18, 22, 27, 37-39, 42-46, 48, 55-57, 61, 63, 67-69, 73-74, 79, 85, 89, 91, 94, 97-99, 104-105
California, v, ix, 2, 4, 6-7, 10-11, 13, 15, 27-28, 48, 69, 71, 94, 97-98, 104
Canadian Coastlines, 16, 34, 42, 63-64, 66, 74, 80, 93, 95
canon, 40
Cardew, Cornelius, 13, 15
CBC, 40
CCRMA, 56-57
CDCM, v, 22, 77, 79-80, 83-87, 89, 91-95, 106
CEMI Event Series, 21
Centaur Records, 22, 77, 89, 91-95, 106
Center for Experimental Music and Intermedia, 17, 21-22, 74, 76, 98
Childs, Barney, 4, 13, 104
Chowning, John, 47, 57

Clark,
  Elizabeth, viii
  Thomas, 4, 8, 22, 66, 69-70, 95, 97, 105
Clementi, Aldo, 13, 15
click-track, 40, 42, 64
Coltrane, John, 59
Computer Music Association, 22, 48, 100-101
concert band, 3, 7, 10, 11, 18, 71
Consortium to Distribute Computer Music, 22, 74, 106 see also "CDCM"
Continuum, 63, 72, 81
conversations, v, 51, 55, 57, 58, 106
convolutions, v, 29, 52, 60, 62-63, 75, 82, 89, 106
Copland, Aaron, 6, 9, 12
Crowley, Timothy, 64
CSound, 48
Cunningham, Merce, 16, 27, 43, 56

Damone, Vic, 6
Dartmouth College, 22
Dashow, James, 48, 91
Davis, 2, 6, 10-15, 17-19, 27-28, 47, 65, 69, 71-73, 98
Debussy, Claude, 9, 53, 75, 82, 89
DEC computer, 19, 47, 48
Denton, viii, x, 2, 16, 20, 25, 42, 48, 56, 58, 71, 73-74, 76
Dido and Aeneas, 30
Distinguished Alumnus, 20, 21, 72
Duke, Stephen, 58, 60, 62, 82, 89-90, 92
Duncan, Oklahoma, 1, 71

Eaton, John, 14, 47
Elliott,
  Bruce, 94
  Paul, 6
Ellis, Merrill, 20, 21
environmental sounds, 50-51, 55, 61
Errante, F. Gerald, 53, 82, 89
Evangelisti, Franco, 13, 15

Floyd,

J.B., 6, 92
Robert, 96
Flux Quartet, 89
form, vi, 8-10, 14, 28-31, 41, 43, 46, 49, 55-56, 65-66, 68
FORTRAN, 47
Foss, Lucas, 13, 27, 67
fractal, v, 39-44, 56, 61, 74, 77, 79,86, 93, 95, 106
Fullman, Ellen, 21-22

gaLarry, 25
Gauldin, Robert, 6
Gause, D., 53
Goetze, Paul, 1
Grundgestalt, 13
Gruppen, 33

Halifax, 40
Harrison, Jonty, 52
Haynie, John, 3
Hehmsoth, Hank, 29
Hewlett Packard, 48
Hiller, Lejaren, 22, 48, 98-99, 104
Hindemith, Paul, 5
Hodges, Johnny, 59, 92
HPSCHD, 48, 98, 104
Hunt, Jerry, 17, 21, 55, 57, 75, 86, 93

I Ching, 24, 37-38
ICMC, 22, 27, 42, 48-49, 56, 100
Imbrie, Andrew, 4, 10, 71
improvisation, v-vii, 4, 12-15, 28, 34, 59, 65, 68, 72, 78-80, 104
Improvisations, 11, 12, 28, 33, 65, 72, 78, 96
International Computer Music Association, 22
International Computer Music Conference, 22, 48, 61, 74, 99, 101-102, 104, see also "ICMC"
International Institute for Electroacoustic Music, 23-24, 75, 85, 91
Ives, Charles, v, 5, 9, 27, 32-39, 67-68, 70, 73, 75-77, 80, 90, 93-95, 97, 102, 106

Jacobs, Paul, 15

Japan, 24, 51, 99
jazz, 2, 3, 6, 9, 10, 11, 12, 13, 28, 33-34, 58-59, 65, 68, 78, 79
Jim Fox Agency, 12
Johnson, Wayne, 17

Kabuki, 23
Kahn, Douglas, 18, 69, 97
Kalve, Martin, 43
Kayn, Roland, 13, 15
Kosugi, Takehisa, 43
KPFA, 40, 57, 92-93
Kubera, Joseph, 53, 81
Kunitachi School of Music, 23
Kurepa,
  Alexandra, 51-52, 91
  Djuro, 51, 91
  Svetozar, 51

LaBarbara, Joan, 44
Large, John, 56
Latham, William, 21
Learning to Compose, vii, 4, 8, 22, 66, 69-70, 74, 97
Lee, William F., 6
Lillios, Elainie, 24, 105-106
Lippe, Cort, 20, 48
linguistic forms, 43
Lowinsky, Edward, 8
Lunetta, Stanley, 6, 13, 15, 17, 69, 98

MIT, 48, 69-70, 105
MacDowell Colony, v, 11, 27, 29-30, 72, 74
Mailman, Martin, 21
Mandelbrot, Benoit, 39-41, 44, 56-57, 106
mapping, v, 39-41, 44
marching band, 3, 7-8, 16
Mathews, Max, 47, 92
Matthews, Michael, 24, 91
McAdow, Maurice, 3
McCormick,
  Mary, 2

Robert, 92

McLean,
  Bart, 21, 27
  Priscilla, 27
Meet the Composer, 57
Mexico City, 24
Michigan State University, 48
Milan, 14
Milhaud, Darius, 4, 7-10, 67, 71
Mills College, 4, 7, 9, 22, 71
Mizelle,
  Dary John, 6, 13,15,17, 106
  Dianne, 44
model, models, modeling v, 4-5, 8-9, 44, 48, 55-56, 61, 66
Moog, 47
Morey, George, 3, 10
Moroles, Jesus, 50-51, 92
Moussorgsky, Modest, 53
Mozart, W.A., 8-9, 24, 29, 53, 75, 82, 89
MSCI 8080, 48
music theory, 5
musicology, 7-8, 16, 71
Musique concréte, 37, 52
Myers, Marceau, 20

National Symphony, 11
Navarro, Edna, ix, 6, 71 see also "Austin, Edna"
New York, vii, 12, 27, 39, 43, 59, 69, 72, 78-79, 81-82, 89-90, 96, 105-106
Newburn, Clarence "Slim", 1
NeXT, 21, 48
Nonesuch Records, 49
North Carolina, 52, 91
North Texas State Teachers College, x, 2, 6, 20, 71 see also "North Texas State University", "University of North Texas", and "UNT"
North Texas State University, 2, 20-21, 48, 73 see also "North Texas State Teachers College", "University of North Texas", and "UNT"
Northwestern University, 48
notation, v, 61, 63-64, 105

octophonic, v, 37, 51, 53-54, 62, 81-83, 85, 90-91, 97
Oliveros, Pauline, 55, 57, 75, 86, 93
omniostic, 45
One O'Clock Lab Band, 2
Open Style, 28, 32-33, 63, 72, 78, 80-81, 84, 87, 96
opera, vi, 2, 27, 30, 56, 87-88
Ortiz, Pablo, 18
Ottman, Robert, 3, 5, 7
Ottuplo, 23, 24, 54-55, 75, 79, 89, 106

Pacifica Foundation, 57
Parker, Charlie, 59
percussion, 3, 4, 34, 77, 92-94
Perspectives of New Music, 16, 70, 99, 101, 104-105
Phelps, James, 24, 106
Pierrot, v, 8, 23, 30-32, 64, 75, 79, 89, 106
Princeton University, 22
Purcell, Henry, 30, 53

Quadrants, 66, 73, 78, 83-84, 86, 88, 92-93, 95

Redux, 52-53, 76, 81
Rensselaer Polytechnic Institute, 22
Roads, Curtis, 48
Robert, Paul, 17
Robson Ranch, viii, ix, 25
Rockefeller Center, 24, 54, 75
Rome, v, 2, 13-15, 28, 39, 47, 65, 72, 83
Rosen, Jerome, 10, 12, 18
Rzewski, Frederic, 13, 15

Saarbrucken, 23, 90
San Diego, 48
San Francisco Composers Forum, 11
Schoenberg, Arnold, 8-9, 31, 34, 67-68
Schuller, Gunther, 11-12, 14
scordatura, 45-46
SEAMUS, 27, 90, 105-106
Serbia, 24

Serra, Xavier 56-57
Sessions, Roger, 7
Sheppard, E. W., 1
Sinfonia Concertante, 8, 29, 33, 74, 77, 95
Smith,
  Julius, 56
  Leland, 47
  William O. (Bill), 14, 47
Smith Quartet, 54, 79, 89
Sonata Concertante, 42-43, 66, 70, 74, 84, 95, 105
Source, v, 7, 9-10, 12-13, 16, 18, 26, 63, 69, 72, 84, 86, 89, 96-98, 103-104
Stanford University, 47, 57
Stern,
  Issac, 12
  Michael, 90
Stevenson, Hamilton, 17
stochastic process, 50
Stockhausen, Karlheinz, v, 15, 17, 33-34, 66-67, 72, 103
Stockholm, 23
Strange, Patricia, 53, 81
Stravinsky, Igor, 31-32
Strawn, John, 42, 48, 69
Subotnick, Morton, 49, 55, 57, 67, 75, 86, 93-94
Swift, Richard, 18
Synclavier, 21, 42, 48, 50
Systems Complex for Studio and Performing Arts, 19, 47, 73, 102

Tableaux, 29, 60, 62-63, 73, 75, 80, 82, 89
Tampa, 15, 19-20, 25, 48, 73
Táragató, 24
tenure, 6, 14, 19, 72
The Netherlands, 23
Thira, 31, 91
Thompson, Michael, 24, 91
Threnos, 30, 63-64, 75, 82, 89-90
Todd, Frank, 6
tonality, 34
Toronto, 40
Trampler, Walter, 44

Truax, Barry, 48
trumpet, 1-3, 5-7, 71
Tudor, David, 15, 37, 43, 55, 57, 72, 75, 86, 93, 96

Universe Symphony, v, 12, 32-36, 38-39, 73, 75, 77, 80, 90, 93-95, 97, 102, 106
University of Birmingham, 23, 75, 91
University of California - Berkeley, 10
University of California – Davis,
University of Illinois, 22, 38, 48, 104
University of North Texas, 2, 20, 22, 42, 72, 74-75, 92 see also "North Texas State Teachers College", "North Texas State University", and "UNT"
University of Michigan, 18, 24
University of South Florida, 19, 47, 73
University of York, 24, 75
UNT, vii, 2, 24-25, 75-76

Varese, Edgard, 52
Vaudelville, 1
Venice, 14, 23, 48, 102
Vercoe, Barry, 48
Vernon, 1, 2, 71

Warsaw, 23
Waschka,
  Andre, 51-52, 91
  Rodney, viii, 91, 104
Williams Mix, 24, 37, 39, 69, 85, 91, 97
Winnipeg, 40
Winsor, Phil, 21
Woodbury, Art, 17, 69, 98
Wuorinen, 19

Yale University, 5, 35-36, 93

ABOUT THE AUTHOR

Thomas Clark's compositions have been performed at festivals throughout the U.S.A., in Canada and Japan, three times at "Moravian Autumn" Brno International Music Festival in the Czech Republic, and at the Festival Internacional Alfonso Reyes in Monterrey, Mexico. Several of his works, affiliated with BMI, are published by Borik Press (based in North Carolina) and recorded on Centaur Records. His writing has appeared in *Perspectives of New Music*, *In Theory Only*, *Computer Music Journal*, *New Groves Dictionary of American Music*, and *Contemporary Composers* published by St. James Press. Co-author with Larry Austin of *Learning to Compose* (1989), Clark wrote an aural development book, *ARRAYS*, published in 1992.

Clark earned a Doctor of Musical Arts degree from the University of Michigan in 1976, where he studied composition with Pulitzer Prize winner Leslie Bassett, electronic music with George Balch Wilson, and conducting with Sydney Hodkinson. He also served as trombonist for Contemporary Directions, Michigan's Rockefeller Foundation supported new music repertory ensemble, and studied elsewhere with virtuoso trombonist Stuart Dempster.

After teaching at the University of Michigan, Indiana University, Pacific Lutheran University, and for 10 summers at the National Music Camp in Interlochen, Michigan, in 1976 Clark joined the music faculty of the University of North Texas. There he developed the New Music Performance Lab and helped develop the Center for Experimental Music and Intermedia, later serving as Associate Dean of the College of Music for 10 years. He now holds the title of Professor Emeritus at UNT.

From 2004 Clark was Dean of the School of Music and Executive Director of the A.J. Fletcher Opera Institute at the University of North Carolina School of the Arts before coming to Texas State University–San Marcos in 2008, where he now serves as Professor and Director of its large, vibrant School of Music.

www.ingramcontent.com/pod-product-compliance
Lightning Source LLC
Chambersburg PA
CBHW032055150426
43194CB00006B/527